RETELLING VIOLENT DEATH

RETELLING VIOLENT DEATH

Edward K. Rynearson, M.D.
Virginia Mason Medical Center
Seattle, WA

BRUNNER-ROUTLEDGE
Taylor & Francis Group

USA	Publishing Office:	BRUNNER-ROUTLEDGE
		A member of the Taylor & Francis Group
		325 Chestnut Street
		Philadelphia, PA 19106
		Tel: (215) 625-8900
		Fax: (215) 625-2940
	Distribution Center:	BRUNNER-ROUTLEDGE
		A member of the Taylor & Francis Group
		7625 Empire Drive
		Florence, KY 41042
		Tel: 1-800-634-7064
		Fax: 1-800-248-4724
UK		BRUNNER-ROUTLEDGE
		A member of the Taylor & Francis Group
		27 Church Road
		Hove
		E. Sussex, BN3 2FA
		Tel: +44 (0) 1273 207411
		Fax: +44 (0) 1273 205612

RETELLING VIOLENT DEATH

1 2 3 4 5 6 7 8 9 0

Printed by Sheridan Books, Ann Arbor, MI.
Cover design by Ellen Seguin.

A CIP catalog record for this book is available from the British Library.
∞ The paper in this publication meets the requirements of the ANSI Standard Z39.48-1984 (Permanence of Paper).

Library of Congress Cataloging-in-Publication Data
Rynearson, Edward K.
    Retelling violent death / Edward K. Rynearson.
        p. cm.
    Includes bibliographical references and index.
    ISBN 1-58391-363-7 (paper : alk. paper)
    1. Death—Psychological aspects. 2. Violent deaths—Psychological aspects.
  3. Bereavement—Psychological aspects. 4. Grief. I. Title.

BF789.D4 R96 2001
155.9′37—dc21

                                                    2001023949

ISBN 1-58391-363-7 (paper)

CONTENTS

PART II
CLINICAL INTERVENTION

PROLOGUE
The Retelling of Violent Dying

A violent death from a suicide, homicide, or accident is more than a death. It is a death caused by an external action. Unlike the internal, impersonal, and invisible dying of disease or wasting, violent dying involves the drama of a fatal human act—someone dies by his or her own hand or the hand of someone else.

The drama of violent dying, though rarely seen, is commonly retold as a story. It is through a story that we describe and understand a series of dramatic events between people. Our minds are accustomed to the structure and function of a story as the telling of human action because we have heard and told action-based stories since we were small children. After the violent dying of a family member, however, the story of the dying may become preoccupying. The compulsive retelling of the violent dying of a family member often eclipses the retelling of their living—the way they died takes precedence over the way they lived. The sustained replay of this dying story becomes unbearable because it can only end in terror. It is this narrative predicament that forces many family members to seek counseling.

Since violent dying is primarily expressed as a story that continues to be retold, this book presents a narrative framework to guide the reader toward a retelling that is restorative. Restorative retelling is the narrative reframing of a violent dying story to include the teller as a participant, rather than a horrified witness, and to reconnect the teller with the living memories of the deceased.

☐ Violent Dying as a Story

I first became aware of the vividness and obstinacy of these stories of violent dying during the Vietnam War when I was training as a psychiatrist. I saw several newly discharged soldiers who could not stop retelling themselves the stories of the violent dying they had experienced and survived.

I was completely unprepared. There had been nothing in my training or reading to guide me in understanding their experiences. I encouraged them to share these stories with the presumption that retelling would somehow "help," and usually it did.

We tried to uncover their feelings. The psychiatric maxim of that era encouraged the release of suppressed feelings—mourning, anger, and guilt—as secondary reactions to a traumatic story. I heard those stories as alien experiences from an alien place, involving the violent dying of buddies, enemies, or civilians. It was obvious that these experiences were horrific, and expressing the anger, shame, and grief that couldn't be allowed while they were soldiers, relieved these young men. As a clinician, I was intent on releasing these soldiers from their overwhelming reactions to these stories of violent death rather than understanding the dynamics of their role in the story.

Those stories of violent dying had a lasting impact. I could not clear my mind for hours after hearing them. Thirty years later, they still blossom as they are rekindled by this writing. Their vividness taught me the power of the story as an early way to search for coherence in chaos. The story structure imposed an orientation to time, place, and plot for those soldiers and for myself as the drama of violent dying was given words.

I knew that these stories were very different than the stories of dying that I was accustomed to hearing from my patients after the natural death of a family member. With natural dying, the story and the feelings focused more on the person and his or her living interaction with the teller than on the story of their dying.

I felt lucky and relieved that my own life had not contained such a story. I was glad to be a listener rather than a teller. That abruptly changed five years later when I was left to retell my own story of violent dying. That was the year my wife, Julie, committed suicide. Her violent dying changed me from an empathic listener to a telling witness.

It is rare that I tell it. After twenty-seven years, the story of her dying has faded and is no longer at the forefront of my memory of her, but it will always be implicit. It is a dark and unwelcome beginning to the way her living was forced from me.

I include my own retelling of Julie's dying in this book in order to present and reframe the story of a violent death and at the same time reveal the personal grounding of my insights. I want to emphasize that this is not a "show and tell" story about Julie or me. It is about her dying and my effort to carry that story forward into my own living. That is more than enough to retell.

It is difficult to begin. Retelling is enigmatic. While the story belongs to me, I was not there when it happened. My retelling of her final moments comes from my imaginary witnessing, which makes my story seem sur-real. It is also painful to retell because I know where it will lead and I don't want to be there at the end.

☐ My Own Story

When Julie first told me that she was afraid that she was going to kill herself, I was sure that she would not. I held her and reassured both of us that she would be all right. It was inconceivable that she would die. Our lives were too young and too bright and were devoted to our two tiny children. There was no time or space for death.

We didn't hesitate to seek help. The psychiatrist met with us that same week and was optimistic. Julie had never been depressed before, and he predicted that she would respond to a combination of medication and therapy. Within a month her depression lifted, carrying away the specter of death. After a few months she saw her psychiatrist less frequently for therapy but remained on medication for a full year.

Her first depression was quickly forgotten. I was focused on building a psychiatric practice in Seattle, she on opening her own Montessori school, and both of us engaged in raising our two preschool children. There was no room for that specter of suicide in the home we purchased on an island close to Seattle, where I commuted each day by ferry.

A year later we decided to have another child. Within months of her pregnancy the depression returned. Her psychiatrist restarted her medication and therapy. Now my reassurance was tinged with apprehension—what would happen if she didn't get better, or if she did, could we trust she wouldn't have a recurrence? She was frightened too; worried that she wouldn't have enough energy for our third child and her new school.

Within days of her delivery, she began to disintegrate. Her despair was increased by her fear that she would fail the children, her business part-ner, and me. We rallied for her. I spent most of the day with the children, her partner hired an assistant, and her psychiatrist saw her more fre-quently for her postpartum depression.

I couldn't deal with my own fear that she might not recover. We met with her psychiatrist to consider how we could keep her safe. Julie prom-ised that she wouldn't kill herself. She knew how horrible that would be for the kids and me. I suggested that she be hospitalized, but she was sure she would feel worse if she were separated from us.

Two weeks later our new baby died suddenly from a brain hemorrhage, and that began Julie's surrender to her depression. She was so guilt-rid-den from her depression that she blamed herself for the death. I was so frightened of Julie's potential suicide that our baby's death was swept into that same dark current. I couldn't separate my grief for our baby from my anticipatory grief for my wife.

I arranged for a leave of absence from work. We tried to maintain a facade of cheerfulness and optimism for each other and the children as we prepared for Christmas, which was only weeks away.

The last time I saw Julie, she was on her way to Seattle to see her psychiatrist. As she backed her blue, Volvo station wagon out of the garage to catch the ferry, she leaned out the window and smiled as she said, *"I've got to finish shopping for the kids, so I won't be back until 4:30."*

By 5:00 when she didn't appear, I left the children with my neighbor and drove to the ferry terminal, dreading what I would find. Her car was in the loading zone in front of the terminal. I caught my breath. I could feel my heart pounding as I parked next to it. Brightly wrapped Christmas presents brimmed the windows. Leaning against her purse on the front seat was a suicide note. The note said she didn't want to die, but she didn't think she was going to recover and she couldn't bear to hurt us anymore. The note was written on the back of her Christmas shopping list with every name crossed off.

As I sat in her car, I constructed in my imagination what she must have done—walked down the passenger ramp and jumped from the moving ferry when it was several miles from shore.

The police helped me radio the ferry captain who was already searching for her. Someone had sighted the apparently lifeless body of a woman floating face down, but by the time they turned the boat, she had disappeared. Her body was never recovered.

☐ Violent Dying as a Private Story

Telling that story still leaves me feeling overwhelmed. At the moment that I opened the unlocked front door of her car and saw her suicide note, I was forced into the awareness that Julie had killed herself. All that I could do was beat on the dashboard of the car and scream, "NO . . . NO . . . NO!"

My story of her dying began with a wailing protest. In those early moments, I could not allow her dying to be happening.

When I first retold the story of her dying to the police and then to our family and friends, I seemed detached from what was happening. I felt forced to retell my imaginary replay of her dying—perhaps as my first "realizing" or giving reality to what had happened. I told it over and over to myself when I was alone. The reenactment of that drama of her dying continued to replay itself in my mind every day and night that first month.

With time and retelling, I became less of a numb witness and more of a participant in her dying story. My mind partially accepted that her dying had happened. Now that the story was "real", my retelling included an imaginary role for myself in the dying drama. By allowing myself a participation in her dying, I began to retell the story from a different perspective. I heard my own voice saying to Julie,

"Don't do this to yourself—or to me."
"Damn it—you promised you wouldn't do this."
"I should have stopped you and protected you."
"I never had a chance to say goodbye to you."

Each of these imaginary voices included me as assertive, angry, remorseful, and finally caring. It was as if my mind let me participate by attempting a dialogue with Julie as she was dying. In giving myself a voice, I wouldn't disintegrate with her in the dying story.

These imaginary dialogues were preludes to a series of stories in which I would try to save her from dying, or rage at her for dying, or blame myself for her dying, or hold and comfort her as she was dying—and there were many more. These imaginary, private stories were woven into a shroud of narratives that surrounded and cushioned the drama of her violent dying. They were interconnected, so I had simultaneous voices and roles to keep me from disappearing into the "black hole" of her dying where she had disappeared.

This shroud of private narratives gave me a sense of separateness from Julie's violent dying, but it was clearly imaginary. So long as the stories remained private, they were mine to construct. They could contain whatever my imagination dictated at the moment I remembered her.

While objective measurements and classification provide a science of the concrete, my narration of Julie's dying attempted a science of my imagination. My imagined roles in these stories allowed me to coexist with her dying in my own imaginary time and space.

☐ Violent Dying Is A Public Story

I could not keep the story of Julie's dying private. The moment I walked into the police station with Julie's suicide note in my hand, her story was no longer mine. Violent dying is the most serious of all crimes and the police and surrounding community demand an open telling. They impose an explanatory story of "who, what, when, where, and why."

There was no role for me in those public stories. The police took her suicide note as evidence in their investigation and within hours, the media was broadcasting and printing the story of her disappearance. The medical examiner and the police were the first in a procession of public agencies determined to retell Julie's dying with a timely and coherent closure. Their retelling was based on an analysis of the concrete facts of her dying in a space and time that could be followed and measured.

They began with the premise of a rational order in her dying that I wanted, but couldn't hope for. I knew that Julie's dying would be a part of my own life story that I would retell long after their stories had been filed and forgotten. Some of the details of the police and media became woven into my private narratives, but they were inconsequential to my retelling.

When their retelling endorsed her dying as suicidal, and not a crime, the media, police, and the court were no longer obligated to retell it. Several months after her death, I regained ownership of my story when the local police chief wrote me a letter announcing the end of his investigation. He enclosed Julie's suicide note as a token of the story's return. Now her dying belonged to me—and to those of us who loved her.

☐ Violent Dying Needs a Restorative Retelling

The continued retelling of a violent death is fundamental to anyone who loved the deceased. For me, the retelling of Julie's violent dying began as a private fantasy, forced to include the more rational and public recounting, and finally returned to me as a memory I carry forward into my own living.

My memory of Julie's life carries the discordant tone of her dying. Whenever I remember the way she died, I am left with a life story that cannot be finished. I'll never be able to tell that story with an ending that is meaningful or instilled with value, because I find no meaning or value in violent death.

I cannot change the ending of her story. The best I can hope for is that I change myself as I retell it. The realization that I need to find a role for myself in her dying story has been the key to restoring myself. That insight changes my perspective from helpless witness, to include who I was before—a husband and friend who did all that I could to help her. This is not the sort of change that magically erases or reverses what happened. The terror and incoherence of Julie's dying isn't dispelled. I will always feel that. But in reestablishing who I was in her life, I am reconnected with my memory of our lives together and that returns me to a time and space of meaning and value. It is this realignment of myself, from "her dying" to "our living," that allows a restorative direction to my retelling.

☐ The Purpose of this Book

Since the purpose of this book is to clarify how to balance oneself above the meaningless void of violent dying, it cannot promise a precise answer. Realigning with the violent dying of a loved one is a dynamic balancing act—like tightrope walking across an abyss, transcending fear and taking small, determined steps toward the end of a rope that stretches into the future. It is a balancing that will be repeated whenever the violent dying is remembered. For as long as I remember Julie, I will find myself balanced over that dark void.

There are too many books on dying and death that promise clarity with the over-simplification that realigning oneself to the death of a loved one is a process that follows discrete stages, ending in a new and enlightened awareness. In my opinion, substituting a bright fantasy of recovery for the dark reality of death is a shallow solution. I can't cite any discrete stages that led to my own recovery after Julie's death. For me, there is no recovery. I can't recover myself when I remember Julie's dying. There have only been two stages—who I was before, and who I am now: changed by her dying.

Instead of recovering, the best I can hope for is an acceptance of how I have changed. Her violent dying continues as a part of my own living because she was a central figure in my life. I am left with the paradox of continuing my own living around my own "reliving" of her dying.

Rather than recovery or answers, this book suggests ways to actively disengage from the futile search for coherence in the imaginary story of violent dying. The way toward mastering a paradox is in understanding that it is irrational. My living and inquiring mind searches for rational and meaningful answers to violent dying, which is irrational and meaningless.

"How could this have happened?"
"How could I have kept this from happening?"
"How can I find retribution for this dying?"
"How can I prevent this from happening again?"

The persistence of this sort of questioning—and then retelling of the violent dying as a story to find an "answer"—is empty and exhausting. This book explains how to disengage from this impoverishment of questioning and retelling, and finally, how to begin and continue a restorative retelling.

☐ The Story Line of this Book

The book begins by engaging the reader in my incoherence immediately after Julie's death. Mired in her dying, my retelling could not include me in that story until I regained my resilience and autonomy from what had happened. My personal retelling gives the reader an illustration of how I, and other family members, can spontaneously begin a restorative retelling.

Coherent retelling avoids searching for a reason or explanation for that intense confusion. None is to be found there. That is why this book puts practice before theory. The first half of the book outlines the development and practice of restorative retelling because it is only after distancing ourselves from the chaos and confusion of violent dying that we can begin its contemplation. The second half of the book clarifies a tentative model of intervention for those who cannot restore themselves spontaneously. The story line of the book in its entirety, progresses from a state of experiential incoherence at the beginning toward a coherent perspective, but not a final explanation or theory.

Part One of the book, entitled Coherent Retelling, outlines how my story, and my telling of Julie's dying, followed a spontaneous, coherent retelling. In Chapters 1 and 2, I describe the availability of inner and outer resources for resilience and show my spontaneous reclaiming of safety after violent dying.

Since retelling is so essential in one's regaining a state of psychological coherence, Chapter 3 describes the narrative, social, biological, and psychological challenges to coherent retelling. These challenges to coherence are important to clarify because they produce exaggerated effects in family members who cannot restore themselves.

Chapter 4 includes the stories of family members who have remained highly distressed and need clinical help. These stories include me as a clinical participant in their retelling. Having served as a psychiatrist and medical director of a specialty clinic that cares for family members after a violent dying, I have shared in many retellings. Since 1984 we have cared for over 1000 family members and have developed interventions that have been applied at other sites and institutions. This chapter engages the reader in the dynamics of practicing what was illustrated in my own retelling.

Chapter 5 closes the first half of the book with a separate consideration of the uniqueness of retelling for children and adolescents after violent dying. Their imaginary and creative ways of coping with violent dying are important to understand before proceeding to the more objective focus of Part Two.

Part Two of the book, Clinical Intervention, presents a framework for helping those who cannot begin their own restorative retelling. Since this book is written for the general reader as well as the clinician, this section of the book outlines a simplified and jargon-free framework for intervention.

Chapter 6 proposes a tentative structure and process to ensure that intervention is coherent and restorative. The essentials of first establishing safety and resilience are followed by an outline of strategies to reinforce them in retelling. The obstacles to restorative retelling (risk factors) are presented along with a recommended screening process for their early identification. The goals of intervention are clearly developed and a guiding procedure to reach them is introduced.

Chapter 7 presents a more detailed description of several group and individual interventions designed for highly distressed family members following the violent death of a loved one. This chapter reviews the empirical evidence of the effectiveness of these interventions and ends with a pragmatic guide to answer the questions commonly posed about the indications for intervention.

Chapter 8 is a selective gathering of the insights of creative investigators of violent dying, beginning with Freud and Janet over a century ago, extending to the original study of violent death—the Cocoanut Grove Fire, then insights on war and genocide, and ending with those of contemporary researchers. This chapter appears toward the end of the book so that these theoretical insights are relevant and enriching to the model of restorative retelling.

Chapter 9 suggests that violent dying is a public health problem with complicated psychosocial determinants and effects. Seen in this context, violent dying becomes a tiny event in its total story. That retelling introduces the social antecedents of violence (poverty, neglect, substance abuse) and suggests that our society promotes violence through its veneration of money and egocentricity as well as its virtual abandonment of children at high risk for violence. A preventive, community-based program for intervention is finally outlined and retrospectively applied to the Cocoanut Grove Fire survivors.

In a concluding section (The Incongruity of Closure) I emphasize the unfortunate connotation of "closure" as a popular and ideal goal in adjusting to death—particularly a violent death. I suggest that restorative attitudes (tolerance for ambiguity and vigilance for novelty) and preverbal unifying images compensate for the meaninglessness and terror of violent dying.

The Appendix includes a description of a systematic assessment, measures for screening co-morbid disorders and written agendas for group interventions.

I

COHERENT
RETELLING

My Own Retelling

First telling my five-year-old son and four-year-old daughter that Julie had killed herself was the hardest telling of all. They had just lost their baby sister, and now their mother. I wondered how I could announce her dying so they could begin to form their own stories. I was afraid that they would somehow blame themselves—as small children often do when a parent dies. I couldn't bear to overwhelm them with more guilt, sadness, and confusion, but they needed to know. I decided that the words I used weren't as important as the attitude we maintained with each other— that no matter what had happened we were going to be safe and we needed to be direct and honest.

I told them what had happened as clearly as I could through my crying. When they began to cry with me, we held each other and I reassured them that we would be O.K. I remember saying that Julie loved us and would expect us to be sad after she died and would want us to be together so we could talk about her and not forget her.

Then I read them to sleep with our favorite bedtime story, *Goodnight Moon*.

After they were asleep I began calling relatives and friends. I told Julie's dying story over and over. Each telling was followed by a reassurance of my strength and optimism—that I would survive her dying. In telling this story of surviving I felt relieved—as if the specter of death had left with her dying.

☐ **The Reenactment Story**

My relief was short-lived. In the days and weeks after her dying, that specter returned. My awareness of her suicide brought such terror and despair that my own survival story was forgotten. Each time my awareness of Julie's suicide returned, it would follow my imaginary reenactment of the last moments of her living. Once the procession of scenes began to unfold, I could do nothing to interrupt. It was like a series of spotlighted scenes drawn from one side of my mind to the other:

> *She walks down the ramp to the ferry and sits alone.*
> *Now that she has written a note, she doesn't want anyone in her way.*
> *When the island becomes a distant margin, she is ready to leave.*
> *She walks to the lower deck and through the parked cars to the stern.*
> *Drawing her brown, wool coat about her, she jumps into the wake.*

Merged in this drama, I would imagine what she thought and felt. This imagining was an endless questioning that wouldn't stop. There was no questioning what she had done, but there seemed no limit to my imagining her last thoughts and feelings.

> *What went through her mind as she stood on the stern?*
> *Was she saying goodbye to the kids and me before she jumped?*
> *Was she welcoming the release of her drowning and the water?*
> *What went through her mind after she jumped?*
> *Was she frightened by the coldness and suffocation?*
> *Did she scream for help because she realized this was a mistake?*
> *What went through her mind as she died?*
> *Did she feel a calmness and transcendence as she became unconscious?*
> *Was she hoping and searching for awareness beyond her dying?*

How could I expect others to understand these imaginary eruptions? I kept them secret, as they kept me from maintaining my concentration during the day and kept me awake at night. I would awake, crying and terrified as I witnessed Julie disappearing in the wake of the ferry. It would take me hours to calm myself so I could get back to sleep. There seemed to be no time or space for my mind to rest.

Now, many years later, I recognize that the reenactment fantasies after Julie's dying were fundamental to forming a story. Seeing and hearing are my primary senses for communicating an experience—with others and my own imagination, as well. The imaginative elements of the story I first fashioned around Julie's violent dying required me to "see" and "hear" what happened. Under ordinary conditions, I recognize some boundary between who I am and what I am imagining. This differentiation allows me to experience the concrete and imaginary at the same time. Under the extraordinary condition of reliving Julie's suicide, I could not differentiate myself from my imaginary story. I saw and heard the reenactment of her dying as if it weren't imagined. In losing myself, I lost ownership of my imaginary story.

In those early weeks after her dying, that reenactment story was so autonomous and powerful that I seemed possessed. Possession suggests that the experience of my imaginary story of violent death at first generated its own energy and drama. Being "possessed" was a helpless experience because I could find no role for myself in the story as it unfolded. At first I could only witness the story. The story needed my voice, but like an oracle, the story came from some source outside my control.

☐ My Fantasy of Julie's Natural Dying

One of the first times that I retold Julie's dying story in a way that included my own voice was when I first imagined how different her dying would have been had she died from a natural cause.

"What if you had died from cancer?"

In that story, there would have been a part for me from the beginning to the end. I would have been there as the possibility of her dying was confirmed by her doctor, and actively involved in trying to save her from death. When the cancer had advanced we could join in preparing ourselves and our kids for her dying. Finally, I would have been there when she died. She would not have been alone. I would have held her and kept her from suffering by herself. Afterward, I could have said goodbye and stepped away. By stepping away, I could release my obligation to protect her, knowing that I had done everything I could.

Her natural dying would have offered a purposeful ending to a story we had constructed together. While she was dying, we might have accepted death on terms that we worked out together. That sort of affirmative ending to her life might be carried forward into my own life story. Participating in Julie's natural dying would have prepared me for my own.

The imaginary story of her suicide left me haunted with the way she had died, with no place or time or ending for me. The imaginary story of her natural dying, on the other hand, brought me the role of active caregiver and I felt relief in secretly telling it to myself.

Unrealized caring seems to be my dilemma. Her dying was so abrupt and isolated, I didn't have a chance to carry out my obligation to protect and care for her while she was dying.

Thereafter, retelling began to contain themes of myself as her protector, even as her savior. These scenarios included desperate but caring acts that I might have done had I been there as she died. I blamed myself for failing to rescue her. I retold myself stories of successfully treating her depression to reverse my failure as husband and psychiatrist. I began to appear in the retelling of her dying as a preserver, racing after her to keep her from jumping. I would rage at her as I pulled her away from the water because she had promised not to leave me this way. These stories added themes of my own remorse and anger in the reenactment. In time, the dramas of my own failure and anger in her dying became almost as painful and possessing as the imaginary reenactment. They were secondary possessions to the reenactment in which I tried to magically reverse her violent dying.

I was so preoccupied with trying to reestablish some sense of order in my own mind and my own home with my children, that I had little energy or receptivity for anything beyond. I know that many things happened in that first month— friends and family converged on us to listen and try to help. This was the first opportunity to retell with those who loved Julie. All they could do was listen and bear witness to me as I numbly recounted what had happened. They had nothing to add.

☐ The Public Story of Her Dying

I remember the first public reporting of her suicide the day after she disappeared. I had hoped for no story at all. Suicide may be a violent death, but it isn't a crime against the public. Why should they need to know? But I was not surprised that it was reported.

December 6, 1974

> *On December 4th the Bainbridge Island Police Department reported the disappearance of Mrs. Julie Rynearson. It is believed that she jumped from a ferry en route to Seattle. A body was sighted by a passenger but not recovered. The Coast Guard searched the area, but no trace of her was found.*

I knew that they didn't need my approval in publishing their story, but I was angry that the reporter hadn't called me before its release. I telephoned the editor to complain. He apologized for their oversight, but reminded me that her death was "a matter of public record" and the newspaper had a right to report it. The story of her dying seemed suspended between us. I wanted to tell him to "back off". So much had been taken from me that this tug of war over the ownership of her story might have escalated. I was so angry that I knew it was safer to say nothing at all. He was sensitive to the tense silence and said what I needed to hear: *"I'm sorry about this—and you have my word that we won't publish again on this story before we call you."*

In a sentence he gave me a role in her story when I could find none for myself.

I was relieved that he never called back. He could not have presented me with a story that I would have found acceptable. There would be nothing in a newspaper story that would help in my own retelling of Julie's dying. I knew more about her dying and her private motivation for killing herself than any reporter could discover and I wanted that to remain private. Their story was only a paragraph. It contained nothing but the barest description of her dying. There was nothing in the story that was inaccurate, speculative, or hurtful. The reporter and editor did their job without interfering with my own retelling. I couldn't have asked for a better public story, though I would have preferred none at all. I suppose that no one remembers the news story but me.

☐ The Riddle of Her Dying

Six months after Julie's suicide, I arranged an appointment with her psychiatrist. By that time my imaginary story of her dying had changed. My possessions of reenactment, remorse, and anger had subsided, leaving me with the puzzle of her decision to kill herself. The inquest of her dying became my private story. Long dismissed by the media and the police, I carried on my own investigation and trial of her dying. I hoped that her psychiatrist and I might arrive at some answers together. After all, he was the last person who had talked with her. Perhaps she had left him with some clue.

Nothing had changed in his office since I had last been there, except the chair beside me was empty. He greeted me with a tight smile and tentative handshake. I told him that the kids and I were doing well, but I had been left with questions about her decision to kill herself. Was there some way we could have stopped her?

He paused as he stared at the ceiling. Without looking at me, he began a recital of the clinical facts and dynamics of her decision to die. I sank, feeling oppressed by this psychiatric autopsy of Julie, told as a clinical story from one psychiatrist to another. We were getting farther and farther from what I had come for.

I asked myself, why? Why wasn't his explanation helping? He was lost in his monologue, determined to answer my question in earnest and logical detail. In my confusion, I realized that he and I weren't going to find an answer with further analyzing. Why couldn't he tell me how badly he felt about her dying? He couldn't feel what I was feeling, but sharing some of his own hurt would have been a more compassionate way to summon our memory of her.

Now he was looking at me, and asked if I had any further questions. I had heard enough. I figured that more questions would lead to a longer monologue. I stood and we smiled and shook hands. His handshake was firmer and his voice more assured as he echoed my opening—that he was glad to hear that the kids and I were doing well and to call if I needed to talk with him again.

I walked across the parking lot outside his office toward the blue Volvo station wagon. It was the same car Julie had driven the last time she left his office. As I sat behind the wheel, I felt myself in the time and place of her decision to die. What was I doing to myself? Was I trying to restore her by following and answering the trail of questions that she couldn't bear to ask any more? I was caught in the dilemma my inquest was creating. I was trying to keep her alive by reversing her dying. In that moment, I realized that I could not begin to restore myself until I stopped myself from trying to save her.

She would not blame me for her dying, which was ultimately her own and not mine.

I left some of that failed obligation in the parking lot as I drove home and began to breathe some life into her memory. Restoring myself meant retelling her living so I could release myself from the ordeal of undoing her dying. The shock of recognizing my over-identification with Julie's dying brought some release from my morbid retelling. I could tell a story that summoned a time and space of her living and that was a story I could live with.

Julie's psychiatrist was not to blame. He was a very caring, and exceedingly competent, clinician who was following my lead. We were both deluded in searching her suicide for an answer—as if her dying was a problem that could be interpreted. Our clinical training as psychiatrists hadn't prepared us to acknowledge that her violent dying was a paradox. The meeting showed me that, like any other bewildered family member after a violent death, I first needed to be reconnected with living. Helping someone after a violent death begins by restoring the living presence of whoever died. I needed Julie's therapist to rekindle our memory of Julie as a valued person whose living was of far more significance than her dying.

☐ Changing Myself in the Retelling

In looking for external answers I was avoiding the fact that her dying was a permanent part of me, that I had to somehow redefine myself around that event. It was hard for me to admit. At first, I was intent on recapturing who I was before—when I felt safe and in control. Unfortunately for my kids, this insistence for constancy began at home. Like most bereaved parents of small children, I was determined to keep our family the way it had been. My kids were probably more aware of this folly than I was able to admit to myself.

One evening the three of us were eating dinner, and feeling drained and empty. I can't remember why I got angry, but it was probably over my cooking. It's hard to enjoy an uninspired meal and they were probably complaining about the food. At any rate, I lost it and yelled, *"Damn it, be quiet and eat!"* They burst into tears and ran from the table. As my anger lifted, I began to recognize how helpless I felt at times like that, without Julie. I started to cry and then began to calm myself so I could retrieve the kids and apologize. My son reappeared, and seeing my tears, crawled on my lap and hugged me. That dissolved me. I was as starved for tenderness as my kids. Hearing my sobs, my daughter peeked around the corner and made a dash for my lap where she wiped my tears and told me "you'll be OK, you'll be OK." Then she tried to read me a story. I'll never forget her telling, for she couldn't yet read, the story of *Goodnight Moon*. She turned the pages and leaned against my chest. I felt a calmness as I relaxed and let them take care of me for a while.

That evening taught me that I had to stop recreating a role that no longer suited the three of us. I would be the best father that I could be, but I couldn't be a mother. I could never bring back the family that Julie took with her when she died. I couldn't be Julie, and couldn't bring back who I was before.

I also needed to stop myself from chasing who I had been. I began to acknowledge that who I am and what I will become is tentative and uncertain. Carrying Julie's suicide within me shapes and shades my vision of my future and myself. Her dying casts an ambiguity and irony over my living and me. I no longer have much patience for absolutes or ultimates.

☐ Reconnecting Julie's Dying with Her Living

Most of my telling and retelling in these early months led to the oblivion of Julie's dying. There were several memorable stories of her living that I heard, but I quickly disregarded them. They were touching, but so unbelievable that I couldn't catch their restorative message.

It began with our laundry man within days of her death. When I answered the doorbell, I could see in his flushed face and watery eyes that he had been drinking again. In one hand he suspended several of Julie's hangered dresses, while the other cradled an unopened bottle of bourbon. He wordlessly handed me the bottle of bourbon, apparently to soften the hurt of the lifeless dresses.

"Doc, I heard what happened. I could tell she was depressed, but we all get that way. She wouldn't do this to you and your children. I know in my heart that she's still alive. She's gone off somewhere to get better—and then she'll come back."

I could smell his leather jacket and the bourbon on his breath as he draped the dresses over my shoulder. He drove off in his battered delivery truck and I never saw him again. I finished the bourbon, but I couldn't finish his story. Her body hadn't been recovered so his drunken speculation was possible. . . .

That same week my four-year-old daughter announced that Julie was "playing a game" with us. She had gone somewhere to hide and she would surprise us by coming back soon, because she missed us. I knew what this story meant to her—a resurrecting of Julie and denying of her death. She told the story for several weeks while I listened. I never challenged her, but reassured her that we would be OK no matter what had happened to Mom. Eventually she stopped telling it, but I couldn't forget her story.

A month later one of my schizophrenic patients told me that he had seen Julie in Seattle. He was in the hospital cafeteria when he overheard two nurses talking about her suicide and he felt very troubled. That same day he saw her crossing a street in front of the hospital. He had never seen Julie before, but there was no question in his mind that she was still alive. I think he felt a mixture of compassion for me and fear that I might die, and telling me that she was still alive would comfort both of us. He never mentioned this sighting again. I recall the story each time that I see him.

I know that this magical thinking is the product of immaturity in my daughter, intoxication in my laundry man, and schizophrenia in my patient. As a physician and a psychiatrist, I demand that my thinking be objective. I don't need to deny dying and death. Julie is dead—end of story. When death happens there is nothing left to tell.

Why then did my mind keep retelling those stories?

My daughter, my laundry man, and my patient were each telling me a restorative message. By logically and narrowly refuting their stories as "magical," I dismissed the transcendence in their telling. In each case, their story of Julie drew me away from her dying and pointed me toward her living memory. The message and magic of their stories is that I can prevail over her dying by finding some meaning and coherence in my living memory of her. Julie is always with me if I let myself remember her.

☐ The Purpose and Path of My Retelling

I believe that my retelling follows a purposeful path in revising my story of her dying. It begins with my engrossment in her last physical and mental movements as she was dying, then includes my own imaginary movements and responses to save and comfort her, and finally detaches me from her dying so I can remember her living. My role in this retelling shifts from my being absorbed and possessed, to involved and participating, and finally, ascendant, while remaining connected to her dying and living memory.

Over time, my retelling becomes less intent on analyzing the truth of her dying, and more open to finding the meaning of her dying in my own life. I won't find truth or meaning for myself in her violent dying, but truth and meaning crystallize and intersect in the evolving story of her dying that I retell. That is the magical effect of retelling—I create truth and meaning by revising myself in the telling.

The purpose and power of retelling comes from reweaving a story with more interconnecting strands of personal truth and meaning. Over time, the enveloping story becomes more like a veil than a shroud—no longer so fixed and concealing. Each time that I remember and retell, I can revise and restore myself, so the darkening of Julie's dying can be lightened.

Resilient Retelling

At first I could barely think or feel.

My mind recoiled. It was as if a physical part of me, like my hand, had been plunged into a hot liquid. With that extraordinary overstimulation, my mind withdrew and protected itself. It felt shut down and, like a badly burned hand, I couldn't work or feel with it.

I could carry on in a detached and muffled consciousness—until the awareness of Julie's dying came. Then my own thoughts and feelings dissolved in my fantasy of her dying. I seemed to oscillate between the extremes of avoiding or becoming lost in her dying.

Retelling a coherent story of violent dying would not begin until and unless my mind established some limits for itself so it wouldn't dissolve in the drama.

☐ The Loss and Return of My Resilience

The mind tunes itself to keep the flow of experience within certain limits. Julie's dying was too much to contain and process. At first it felt like her dying would explode me, with all the neurons in my brain firing at once. My mind needed restraints and boundaries to protect itself from the cascade of too much pain.

This capacity to maintain experience within tolerable limits is what I call *resilience*. Resilience is a dynamic, mental reflex that is implicit and imperceptible. It is difficult to recognize and define because the awareness of a reflex comes with its insufficiency. I can't appreciate resilience until I try to use my mind without it. Resilience screens and sculpts experience through a reflexive selection that is as coordinating for my mind as the more familiar neurologic reflexes that coordinate my balance and movements while running or stepping off a curb.

Don't let anyone persuade you that avoidance is unhealthy. Resilience first allowed me a temporary avoidance from the chaos of Julie's dying. In the immediate experience and aftermath of overwhelming trauma, it was essential. When my mind first disintegrated in the awareness of her dying, all I could do was scream, "NO . . . NO . . . NO!" Avoidance was my only option.

Later, I no longer actively avoided an awareness of her dying. Resilience brought constancy for me in the dying awareness, keeping me calm from what I felt and separate from what I thought. Now I could engage with my dying fantasy. Resilience first brought a barrier and then a transcendence that protected me from over reacting. It was as if my resilience was saying, *"Wait a moment—try not to think or feel your way out of what's happening. You're going to survive by staying on the surface. Flow with this until you can master it. Don't lose yourself by resisting and struggling."*

That resilient image, "float and flow," came from an experience I had when I was twelve or thirteen and first swam in the ocean. I wasn't used to the surf and I remember the exhilaration of pulling myself out of that first wave that crashed around me. As the day progressed, I grew more confident—that by swimming and launching myself over their crest I could ride waves as they sped me toward the beach. But I knew nothing about undertows, and I remember thrashing and gasping against a strong, hidden current that swept me past and beyond the other swimmers. Now I was not only exhausting myself with my futile swimming for shore, but also beginning to panic. Thankfully, the undertow spent itself—as it always will—and I began to wearily swim toward the beach. A lifeguard, who came out to help, swam back with me.

As we sat on the beach, he insisted on talking before I began body surfing again.

"If you're going to swim in the ocean, it's more important to remember how to float than to know how to swim."

He was reminding me how we all learned to master ourselves in the water before we began swimming. By floating on my back, with my face out of the water, I could float and flow with any current.

That lesson has served me well in strong currents of every kind. Mastering an overwhelming force may begin by "floating and flowing"—keeping me safe and buoyant until I regain control. It is altogether different than surrendering where I am helpless. Instead, I choose to be swept in its energy to conserve my own.

Resilience tells me to survive by floating and flowing on the surface of my awareness of Julie's dying. The "keeping" of resilience brings an ability to distance myself from both the reality and my fantasy of her dying—from the enormity of her dying and its distortion in my fantasy.

The early return of resilience was fundamental to my retelling.

It began the night of her dying when I reassured my children, and later my friends and family, that I was safe and confident I would survive. I needed to repeat that reassuring story to divert myself from the void of her dying. There was a resilient voice for all of us in the reassuring story of our mutual survival (Pennebaker, 1990).

One of my close friends told me he admired my confidence and optimism, but he was tired of hearing me retell it. He suggested that there was more to my story than I was admitting. We smiled at my unspoken story of helplessness, but he didn't insist that I tell. He was a good friend and wasn't confronting, but rather announcing his willingness to listen to a "fuller" story—and he did.

In that first month my mind, like a badly burned hand, needed time to heal. Fortunately, my resilience was durable and available. I can't suggest a mechanism for its return beyond its own regeneration over time. When it first returned it was forced and clumsy, announcing itself in my too-strident story of survival. Gradually, resilience began to center my mind so I could retell a story around the nothingness of her death and the meaninglessness of her dying.

Those early weeks of intrusion and possession illustrate how crucial resilience is as a resource of stability. Summoning the confidence that my mind could survive the fact and fantasy of Julie's dying was foundational. Retelling and restoration were based on it. When someone can't restore them self after a violent dying it is because they can't remain resilient.

☐ External Resources for Resilient Retelling

My resilience began privately, but it needed to be nourished and reinforced within my family and community. Fortunately, there were several collective resources.

At first I found resilience by acting resilient. I was so determined to provide resilience for my children, to protect them from further trauma, that my own needs for resilience were enacted with them. That is the way that many family members, particularly parents, begin their own resilient retelling—by mutually retelling a story that promises that the family will survive the violent dying together. This mutual enactment of reassuring calmness and confidence between my children and myself had its rough moments. There were times when we couldn't deny how badly we felt—no matter how hard we tried to take care of each other. And I had to accept those times as inevitable to our retelling rather than as a personal failure.

I kept Julie's memory alive between us and would refer to her often. I found resilience for myself in recalling how strong and competent she had been as a wife and mother. The children listened to my remembrances, but rarely spoke of her spontaneously after the first several months. I suppose they were as concerned about my safety and stability as I was about theirs—and it was less threatening for the three of us to retell a story of our future as a family than our past. She had been a devoted and caring mother for them, and I shared their bewilderment in her abandonment. We were cut off and adrift from Julie's decision to leave us. We couldn't resolve the way she had ended the story of our family.

My own experience of enacting resilience with my children suggests that resilience is communicated more by actions than words. We couldn't exist in the story her dying had forced on us—and we couldn't retell it with words that would bring safety or meaning. Instead, we found reassurance in unspoken behaviors and habits of resilience such as soothing, holding, and assurance of proximity. We were separated when I was at work, but spent all of our evenings and weekends together. I wanted my kids at home, with me, so I invited their friends to spend time with us. On weekends our house was in a perpetual state of social excitement and laughter. All three of us were buoyed by the gaiety, but I was relieved when the others left and we were by ourselves again. With only three of us, our togetherness was palpable. Resilience came in being unified and knowing that we would be constant for each other.

My Work

There was nothing self-sacrificing in returning to my work as a psychiatrist. I felt lost without it and couldn't wait to get back. I also felt an obligation to return for my patients and my associates, and an even stronger need for resuming my role as a doctor that was stabilizing and satisfying. Staying at home made me too aware of Julie's absence. Being at work not only allowed me to continue being resilient for others, but diverted my mind. In those early months, I did not look forward to periods of solitude that forced me to be introspective. The private time and space of my mind was not where I wanted to be.

Work was not a place where I retold Julie's dying. I wasn't open with my patients. Several of my long term therapy patients found out about her death and I was candid in answering their direct questions, but they were uncomfortable in listening. My associates were sensitive to what I was weathering, but they rarely asked and I rarely talked about her dying.

My return to work provided a familiar context of purpose and meaning where I could find resilience for myself in caring for others. I was stoic and unperturbed at work, because my action as a physician recreated an order and predictability in my living to counterbalance my unspoken immersion with dying. Work brought resilience by reengaging me with life.

Spiritual Beliefs

There are times when I am sorry I don't have a strong spiritual or religious belief. A concept of order after death has been stabilizing for humankind for thousands of years. Sharing such a belief with a community of fellow believers brings a comforting reassurance that dying can be understood in living terms. Life after death or reincarnation would promise that Julie had not disappeared and I could anticipate a reunion with her after my own death.

Julie and I had talked about dying and death and she had a strong spiritual belief in her continuity. She was confident that she would continue to exist in some indefinable way after death and was comforted by that anticipation. Knowing she had that hopeful attitude as she died softened my fantasy of her last moments—but I could find no resilience for myself in her belief.

While religious and spiritual concepts might have prepared me for Julie's death, they could not prepare me for her violent dying. There is no spiritual belief or religion, despite any scripture or hymn or sermon that finds order or meaning in a violent death. When a fireman, policeman, or soldier dies violently, the story of their dying isn't told. Their dying is muffled by repeated testimonials of their bravery and sacrifice in protecting the rest of us. Their violent death is transformed into a dying emblematic of their selfless choice to stand in harm's way and die in honor.

But honor comes from the courageous choice of self-sacrifice. Violent dying by itself cannot be transformed into a meaningful or courageous choice. Homicidal or accidental dying is a transgression rather than a choice, and Julie's suicide was a transgression against my children and me since we had no part in accepting her choice.

Julie's memorial service was designed to celebrate her life. Any mention of her dying was avoided. I remember the great outpouring of love for Julie, but a numbing disregard for what her dying had done to us. It would not have helped to stir our fantasies of her dying. We needed to gather to be resilient for one another while we began to retell a shared story of her life. Being reminded of her living was a resource of resilience for all of us.

☐ Resilience as a Foundation

After Julie's suicide my first challenge was to mentally survive my fantasy of her dying. My familiar awareness of my surroundings and myself was lost in the turbulence of avoidance and intrusion, so my first priority was to recover enough resilience that my mind would find some limits and coherence.

The early resource of resilience came from my enacting a survival story for myself and my children that I told and performed repeatedly. This early story contained an idealistic fantasy that I felt compelled to retell to counterbalance the annihilative fantasy.

I first found resilience in being resilient for others—initially for my family and later for my patients. I also had my private mantra of resilience—float and flow—that I would summon as a comforting image or place for myself when I was overwhelmed. Private images of safety and transcendence are powerful nonverbal stabilizers. I was barely aware of my own, until Julie's dying.

Resilience is directional—it points towards living—so I became a survivor of violent dying by first surviving. My family, my friends, and my work reconnected me with being resilient and alive. It was only after my mind was re-anchored in living that I could be resilient for myself.

The return of resilience brought enough calmness and confidence in living that I could coexist with Julie's dying. I could not have spontaneously resumed or fully participated in my living and my life without it. If my mind, like a hand with a third degree burn, could not have recovered its inherent resilience, I would have remained numbed and, finally, disabled. My mind would not have restored itself by forming an enlivening awareness around the annihilation of Julie's dying, and I would have stayed deadened.

From Incoherent to Coherent Retelling

My retelling followed a purposeful path, from an early immersion and loss of my own boundaries in Julie's dying, to a resilient redefinition and reengagement of myself in living. This shift in the narrative focus, from the incoherence of her dying to a reconnection with my own living, retold a story that could be revised.

The vast majority of friends and family members who have been overwhelmed by the violent death of a loved one spontaneously arrive at a coherent and restorative retelling. Like me, they are possessed with the dying for several weeks or months and then, with resilience and the support of their family, work, and community, accommodate themselves around this tragedy.

A minority of survivors cannot make this narrative shift. They can't stop retelling the violent dying. I recognize this immobility because I felt paralyzed by the same retelling in myself. There is nothing distinctive in their story of reenactment or possession. It has the same vivid form and plot, but cannot be revised. Remaining possessed and "stuck" in this morbid retelling for months or years begins to suck life from the teller.

☐ The Incoherence of Killing and Caring

There is an inherent instability in the very structure of the dying story that complicates its retelling. Its structure cannot contain the simulta-

19

neous dramas of killing and caring. The action of violent dying disinte-
grates the linear drama of caring.

Because of its instability, the narrative structure of violent dying is spheri-
cal and pulsating rather than linear and static. The contradictory dramas
of violent dying and protective nurturance are central images that alter-
nate and spin off secondary dramas. There is such disparity in the intention and direction of these two imaginary dramas that they cannot be
joined in the same telling.

Initially the reenactment of the dying image is at the very center and
stories of remorse, retaliation and protection are secondary themes that
tightly surround it. These are compensatory dramas that are directly related to the violent dying.

Later, reenactment is counterbalanced by a living image of the deceased
tightly surrounded by fantasies of reunion and restitution. These are compensatory dramas that are directly related to the primacy of the caring
relationship but stifled by the isolation and immediacy of violent dying.

Still later, both imaginary dramas and their secondary dramas will become dimmer and less central, though if triggered, may immediately return in their absorbing replay and conflict.

With any death, the theme of reenactment will be narrated before any
other. If two people meet and one begins to tell the other of the death of
someone they both know, the story begins with the way that person died.
In the story of the dying, that person still lives and the dying drama describes the action in resisting or accepting the inevitability of death.

The narrative structure of a natural dying story is a linear replay of a
dying that may include the time and attention of many. There is an inherent reconstructive direction in this story as it progresses towards a sad,
but resigned, acceptance that death at least may bring an end to pain or
helplessness. With natural dying, the reenactment story contains a complex plot that allows many participants to fashion a story together. They
gather around the dying family member to prevent or prepare for death.
When death finally comes with natural dying, ideally each family member has an opportunity to engage in a final role as comforter and protector so whoever dies will not die alone.

The narrative structure of violent dying is spotlighted killing. In this
horrific action of the violent dying no one prevents or intervenes in the
killing. Unlike natural dying, the story of violent dying does not contain a
reconstructive potential because this is a dying that cannot be mutually
accepted or softened. With violent dying, the deceased and the family are
isolated from one another by a rush of action that does not allow a collective attempt to prevent or prepare for death. There is no opportunity to
gather and create a dying story together, or even be there as the family
member is dying. When death happens violently, the family member has

no role beyond that of passively witnessing a dying action they can't stop themselves from imagining.

Since the story of violent dying lacks reconstructive direction or potential and is traumatically isolated from the life-affirming narrative of caring and protection, it cannot be changed. It can be relentlessly repeated, but not enlivened or retold with a perspective that transcends the dying drama. This narrative dilemma, retelling a story that is a structural dead end, fundamentally complicates retelling. It doesn't help to repeat a story of senseless disintegration and nihilism. There is an implicit ruination that no one who retells can escape.

Family members are left with a final narrative dilemma of joining this story of violent dying to the story of their own life. Violent dying is not only a tragic and unacceptable ending to the life story of the deceased, but is carried forward as a chaotic and unacceptable ending of vitality and identity in the continuing life story of the teller (Frank, 1995; Harvey, 2000; Neimeyer & Levitt, 2000). Retelling this broken life-narrative cannot be seamless, because the life of the teller in that shared narrative has ended as well. When a loved one dies violently, the nurturing connection with the memory and future life of the deceased remains torn and ingrained. To reconstruct a narrative of living from a violent dying that is deeply embedded is paradoxical. The violent dying story begins with a brief drama, but that beginning is endless. After the violent death of someone we loved, our life story is destabilized, because living may encompass but cannot extinguish the pulsing sphere of the dying memory.

☐ The Mandates of Violent Dying: The 3 V's

Each violent dying occurs as a drama. Three dimensions within that drama distinguish violent dying:

> **Violence** — The act of dying is injurious.
> **Violation** — The act of dying is transgressive.
> **Volition** — The act of dying is willful (suicide or homicide) or an irresponsible negligence (most fatal accidents are due to human error).

These **3 V's** (violence, violation, and volition) are ingredients of a human act that transform the dying into something abhorrent. This sort of dying is unacceptable. Someone is killed. The family and community are frightened and outraged, not only by death, but the potential that this dying might happen again. It should have been avoided—it was someone's fault.

The mandate for retaliation, retribution, and punishment is an inherent counterstory to the 3 V's of violent dying. The action of a violent dying must be revenged, for both the family and the community. For the family, the sanctity of an irreplaceable life is lost in the violence of the dying, and whoever died must be avenged by a reciprocal drama to restore their honor and respect. For the community, the sanctity of its own order and peace has been threatened, and whoever is responsible must be found, restrained, and punished. The three V's require a ritualized retelling of the dying to construct this mandatory counter drama. This ritual promises to restore moral order for the family and legal order for the community.

Social Mandate

For thousands of years humans have killed themselves or others for all manner of selfish and noble purposes. We are more capable of killing ourselves than any other species and perhaps we respond to violent dying with such intensity because of its potential in our own nature.

In preliterate times, before written laws or criminal-judicial agencies, families would gather as a clan to construct and carry out their own revenge and retribution. "An eye for an eye and a tooth for a tooth" offered an action of reprisal in which the killer was forced to die in the same way that the family member had been killed, or the family of the perpetrator would offer some tangible retribution, called "blood money." This ritual of mandatory revenge or retribution may have enacted a crude return of morality and order, but it must have been enormously disruptive. Presumably, that is why violent dying became a "crime against the King" in Twelfth Century England. The monarchy would not tolerate the social and economic turmoil stirred by these clan practices.

Since that time, in Western society the family has lost any meaningful role in this compensatory drama. Instead, the agencies of the police and court follow an increasingly complex system of rules and procedures. Few outside the agencies can readily understand or follow what happens.

Though these laws have transformed revenge and retribution into an objective investigation and a trial that respects the ideals of individual rights and justice, it has sapped the mandatory counter drama of its directness. Of course, revenge is still practiced by individuals and families who circumvent the lawful system, but at great risk of being charged with homicide themselves.

The three V's mandate a social appropriation of the violent dying by the medical examiner and the police until it is legally established as a crime. Intentional homicide and vehicular homicide are considered criminal and are mandated to the state. Accidental and suicidal dying are not, and the family is left to retell their own mandatory story.

The police and court serve the law more than the family.

Private Mandate

Family members carry out their own investigation and trial independent of the police and court. The three V's of violent dying have a private arena and agenda within the mind. Family members may be preoccupied with an imaginary inquiry and judgment that churns beside, and beyond, the police and court. In some minds it can be as powerful as the story of reenactment and it is not obligated to follow a lawful path.

Crime or no crime, with violent dying the family member needs to inquire how and why the dying was allowed to happen. This private inquiry and judgment can be possessing while generating its own conclusion. It may find the teller accused "guilty of a failure to protect" and demand a sentence of lifetime *remorse* as self punishment, or a self-imposed "mobilization" as *protector* to guarantee the safety of the remaining family, or an "ordeal" of *retaliation* to find and punish someone else.

Unfortunately, within this possessing inquiry and trial, there is no protection of rights or assurance of justice for the teller. Since the proceedings are internal and closed, there are no voices to speak for the defense. When possessed, family members cannot see their private investigation and trial as unjust and unbalanced. It is unfortunate that they can't be read their rights—a Miranda Rights for Self Accusers—that advise them to remain silent to avoid self-incrimination.

☐ Connection and Retelling

The highly responsive family has a strong nurturing link between its members, and it is this connection that maintains mutual concern and protectiveness. When this shared concern and protectiveness is absent, a violent death may have little impact. The potential for connection may have withered from neglect or disintegrated from rage and abuse. When a violent death involves someone who led a life of extreme neglect or violence within the family, their violent dying may occasion more relief than grief. In the absence of a caring connection, a violent death cannot create something from nothing. Highly dysfunctional families without trust and concern for one another lack a reservoir of connective memories to summon a mandatory response to the three V's. The remnants of connection are so crisscrossed with self-protective barriers that whomever was killed was not valued or seen as deserving of concern or protection.

Such an extreme circumstance of family disconnection is rare, but shows the necessity of a caring connection for retelling. Without caring there is little impetus to retell the dying or living story. Most of us are aware of this disconnection in ourselves in our daily exposure to violent death. We are bombarded by media reports of violent dying which have little impact beyond our being alarmed by the killing. These dramas catch our attention, but usually involve someone we don't care for or about. That someone is not a part of our personal time or space. While the brief spectacle of their dying may be engrossing, the three V's of their dying stirs little imaginary reenactment or possession.

The mandatory three V's are reserved for the violent dying of those who are connected through shared memories of caring. Since the caring connection is fundamental to retelling, it is not surprising that of all family members, parents are most vulnerable to reenactment and possession. Parents, and particularly mothers, may have a prolonged and painful response to the violent death of their child, whatever the age (Rosenblatt, 2000). The role of a parent involves an ultimate obligation to protect the child from harm. When the child is killed it is most often the parent who feels disproportionate shame. It is difficult to divert a parent from the mandatory rite of self-investigation and trial, which may include the wish that he or she had died violently instead of the child. The duty of parental obligation makes parents more responsive to a violent death than other family members including children, siblings, or spouses. This probably explains why mothers and fathers are the family members who most frequently ask for support and treatment after a violent death.

☐ The Incoherence of Intense Distress

The death and violent dying of an emotionally valued person is an external and indirect threat. It is rare that someone distressed over a violent death was at risk of his or her own violent dying. Instead, the distress is provoked by the persistent memory of the vulnerability of the person as he or she was being killed. Distress after the violent dying of a loved one is a mental and physical response that diminishes as the threat subsides. However, because of the caring connection, the external event of violent dying is transformed into an internalized memory of the killing. So long as this combination of the killing memory and the caring obligation remains, the distress response to violent dying continues.

There are two distinct, but intertwined, distress responses to violent death: Death creates *separation* distress to the irreversible loss of the person, and violent dying creates an additional *trauma* distress to the way the person died.

The following table shows that the distress responses of separation and trauma are roughly separable into specific thoughts, feelings, and behaviors.

	Trauma Distress	Separation Distress
Thoughts	Reenactment	Reunion
Feelings	Fear	Longing
Behavior	Avoidance	Searching

Each distress response has a specific psychological purpose as well. Separation distress is intent on reestablishing a psychological and physical connection with the living presence, while trauma distress is intent on replaying and avoiding the dying presence. Both are rudimentary efforts to master the combined effects of death and violent dying.

The thoughts, feelings, and behaviors of simultaneous separation and trauma distress are not harmonious. Separation distress draws toward an embracing reunion with the person's vitality, while trauma distress dreads and avoids the imaginary witnessing of the person's dying. Separation and trauma distress enact contradictory dramas with the memory of the killing. One response pulls toward, while the other pushes away, the memory of the deceased.

These dramas of distress are so contradictory that it is difficult to consider them at the same time. At first, trauma distress takes precedence. The numbness, avoidance, and reenactment fantasies of trauma distress all but extinguish the longing, searching, and reunion fantasies of separation distress. Perhaps trauma distress is more powerful because it serves a more essential survival purpose. For thousands of years our central nervous system has prepared us to avoid before approaching death. The tendency of approach and avoidance surrounds death, but there is an inherent tendency to first avoid before approaching violent death. Our central nervous system is programmed to process the trauma of violent dying before the more complex reprocessing of the emotional connection with the deceased.

Trauma distress and separation distress are not isolated from one another. Both are potential at any time. In those early weeks and months after a violent death, trauma distress subsides to be gradually replaced by separation distress that can now approach the memory of the person as well as their killing.

The simultaneous occurrence of trauma distress and separation distress after the death of a family member is illustrated in a hypothetical diagram (Figure 3.1) that visualizes their shared expression over time.

In my experience, this dimensional model of distress is more valid than the model of stages. The stage model suggests a series of discrete emotional responses that follows a predictable order—as if one stage builds on

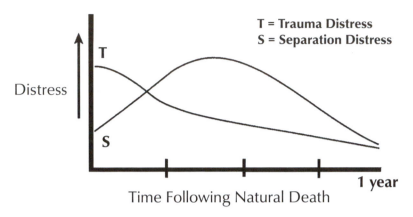

FIGURE 3.1. Trauma distress and separation distress after natural death.

the one preceding it. This model of discrete, unfolding stages makes the mistaken assumption that recovery somehow follows this same sequence.

Instead of stages, the dimensional model suggests that trauma distress and separation distress are simultaneous responses that vary in intensity over time. There is no first stage. Numbness is associated with intense trauma distress rather than a separate, categorical stage. The numbness and shock of bereavement follows our inherent fear and avoidance of death. The fear of death continues as a potential response that may recur. Though separation distress becomes more predominant over time, trauma distress cannot be extinguished or forced away. With the dimensional model there is no fundamental transformation from one stage to another. Trauma distress and separation distress are deeply embedded responses that have been stirred, rather than caused, by the death of a family member. They are distress responses that remain implicit and are widely connected with multiple experiences, not only death.

Figure 3.2 is a hypothetical visualization of the interplay of trauma distress and separation distress after a violent death.

With violent dying, trauma distress is more intense and sustained. It continues for several months, instead of diminishing within weeks as it would with natural death. A significant minority of family members, perhaps 30% of parents (Murphy, 1999), suffer persistent thoughts of reenactment, remorse, retaliation, and overprotection, for years instead of months, and their "possession" is represented by the dotted line.

This finding of prolonged and intense trauma distress associated with possession after a violent dying is a risk factor. Those who remain immobilized in their trauma distress have difficulty in reengaging with their

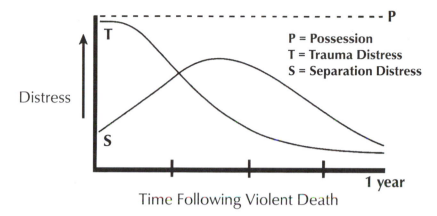

FIGURE 3.2. Trauma distress, separation distress, and posession after a violent death.

living. They behave as if the killing had just happened. In the private space and time of their traumatized awareness, the violent dying cannot be relegated to the past. Days and nights bring intrusion of reenactment fantasies in vivid immediacy. The violent dying keeps recurring as a "right now" experience despite the passage of time.

There is no time for the future. It is difficult to reengage with living when the mind is so intent on merely surviving the immediate ordeal of the reenactment or the possessive dictates of remorse, retaliation or protection. The internalized memory of the killing cannot be consigned to past memory, so it continues to generate traumatic distress.

☐ The Incoherence of Avoidance and Possession

It is the absolute absence or intrusion of the dying memory that interferes with restorative retelling. With avoidance, the retelling cannot begin. With possession, the retelling cannot stop.

It is easier to recognize possession because of its vivid awareness. Avoidance evades awareness, but it can be as "deadening" as possession. When avoidance becomes too intense there is a numbness and disregard for engagement.

Avoidance

When an overwhelming stress, like violent death, occurs in someone with a comparatively consistent life history and available resilience, avoidance may be adaptive. It is misleading to suggest that avoidance is permanent and irreversible in someone who rarely uses it. Avoidance of the awareness of violent dying is a natural first response that provides mental stability before resilience is reestablished. Avoidance deserves respect, until it can be replaced with a more resilient response.

It is difficult to give an operational definition of avoidance because its "operation" is to render existence into nonexistence.

Avoidance is a more primary mental reflex than resilience. Rather than calming and separating the mind from the awareness of violent dying, avoidance disavows any emotional impact. Unlike denial, a more immature reflex that altogether erases the awareness of the violent dying (and is more commonly operative in small children), avoidance acknowledges that violent dying happened, but refuses to acknowledge its associated trauma and grief distress. While avoidance may serve an immediate protective function, it is an artificial solution. Avoidance is a common response in the immediate aftermath of an overwhelming trauma, but eventually resilience replaces avoidance with an emotional awareness that can be processed and revised.

There is a virtual absence of developmental research on avoidance. It cannot be actively observed or reported. Those who habitually avoid are not aware of avoidance or associated distress.

Mental health clinicians recognize that individuals who have suffered a high degree of childhood abuse and neglect over utilize avoidance. This intuitively fits. Since avoidance is so primary in protecting the mind, it would take precedence over resilience when a child is repeatedly abused. Many adults who were forced to survive such a childhood are permanently disabled. Though excessive avoidance allowed their mental survival, it maintains an attitude of emotional detachment, and, like automatons, they survive life without joy or sadness or empathic engagement. They may create an artificial aura of resilience by "numbing" themselves through frantic over-activity or substance abuse. After a violent death, they are intent on shielding themselves from what happened. They so avoid the awareness of violent dying that they hardly recall that it happened.

Possession

Like avoidance, possessive thoughts are a common first response to violent dying. Their appearance is a rudimentary accompaniment to the processing of the dying memory and should not be interpreted as abnormal. However, when possessive fantasies of violent dying do not spontaneously diminish, the teller becomes a helpless witness or subject within the awareness, having lost governance of himself or herself.

Possessive fantasies are roughly separable into categories:

1. The primary fantasy contains the **reenactment** of the dying itself. Retelling this fantasy makes no reference to the teller, other than as helpless witness.
2. The secondary fantasies contain a compensatory theme of **remorse** (i.e., "I should have prevented this from happening"), **retaliation** (i.e., "someone else needs to pay for what happened") or **overprotection** (i.e., "I will not allow this to happen again"). These secondary fantasies refer to the teller as blameworthy, retaliatory or protective, and each of these roles imposes an obligatory duty. The blameworthy must punish themselves, the retaliatory must find and punish someone else, and the overprotective must guard themselves and their loved ones from what has happened.

This rough categorization of possession into primary (reenactment) and secondary (remorse, retaliation, and protection) themes points to the relative prominence of possession. In someone with diminished resilience who is "possessed," the primary and secondary themes may shift and merge as they tightly encircle the awareness. However, in every possession or in any combination, the violent dying continues to energize the retelling.

☐ The Biology of Resilience and Memory

The awareness of a violent dying as a story, and of our resilience in retelling, has a neurobiologic basis. While each story and retelling is private, it occurs in an organic system, our brain. The human brain is so wondrously complex that it can adapt itself to changes from without or within, but there are fundamental limitations in its capacity to perceive and process a trauma like violent dying.

While there is evidence that our heredity and development have a lasting impact on our capacity to adapt to trauma, resilience is expressed through neurobiologic mechanisms. In all probability, diminished resilience, avoidance, and possession are descriptions of altered mental states that may be secondary to, or reflected by, specific "alterations" in the neurological processing of traumatic memories. There is a recent, readable review (Damasio, 1999) of the physiology of consciousness that describes these mechanisms in detail.

Neuropsychiatry researchers have measured chemical, structural, or functional changes in the brains of subjects who remain traumatized for many years—particularly in groups of Vietnam War veterans. There are some promising findings, changes in the activity of areas deep within the brain that are associated with states of intrusion and avoidance. These studies substantiate what we have long suspected. For decades it has been presumed that the disordered activity of these areas, the amygdala and hippocampus, were associated with persistent traumatic responses. However, these changes and their measurement are of no clinical utility. At this time, there is no neurochemical or neuroimaging study from this research that helps the clinician or traumatized family member. Our brains undoubtedly influence and are influenced by the traumatic memory of a violent death, but the more subtle influences cannot be measured by these relatively crude studies.

Presumably, the neurobiologic mechanisms underlying the restorative or nonrestorative retelling of the violent dying of someone we loved would involve multiple memories and areas of association—for they would be deeply registered within our brain.

There is a neurological system of memory registration, storage, and retrieval underlying the experience of the memory of a violent dying. Neuropsychological researchers have identified independent memory systems which function beyond our awareness. Each of these memory systems, called semantic, episodic, or procedural, has been roughly localized to different areas of the brain. Semantic memory is primarily symbolic and verbal (e.g., words and calculations), episodic memory is multisensory and preverbal (e.g., intense experiences of pleasure or pain), while procedural memory involves acquired skills and emotional and physical reactions that have no words (e.g., riding a bike, aversion to certain colors, noises, or smells). Under normal circumstances, an experience can be selectively processed, registered, and stored in one or a combination of these memory systems.

Intense trauma somehow alters this selective processing so the memory becomes fragmented and abnormally registered. The neurobiologic details of this altered processing remain obscure; however, recent radioisotope and neuroimaging studies have demonstrated an area of the brain (the amygdala) that appears to serve as an emotional "control center" activated by excessive emotion, including intense fear, and through its connections with other areas of the brain (the hypothalamus, brainstem, and frontal cortex) produces a sustained state of hypervigilance and arousal.

Amygdala activation is also associated with an incomplete processing of traumatic memory, presumably secondary to its connections and effects on the cerebral cortex. There is a delay in the registration of traumatic experience as semantic memory. It is first perceived as a vivid, multisensory episodic memory that is recalled as an intrusive, wordless flashback or may register at a procedural level of memory where there is no conscious recall.

The neurobiologic model of memory selectivity suggests that semantic, verbal memory provides the most accurate and integrated representation of the trauma experience. This parallels the universal and timeless practice of people needing to put words to troubles. To symbolically process a traumatic event through words somehow encourages the conversion of the experience into semantic memory. Since semantic memory offers a continuum of time and space, the experience can be encoded as an external event that occurred in the past. The activity of talking and listening may transform a traumatic experience, as a semantic memory that can then be released and recalled at will.

This description of the neurobiologic foundation of traumatic memory is necessarily simplified and speculative. For our limited clinical purpose it is better to highlight several mechanisms of altered recall and registration of traumatic memory of violent dying.

Another significant neurobiologic factor that influences retelling is the presence, or *comorbidity*, of one or several psychiatric disorders. A psychiatric disorder is different than distress. Disorder implies a relatively autonomous, neurobiologically-driven syndrome that may occur without any external threat. While distress is associated with a specific, stressful experience (and its persistent memory), a psychiatric disorder may begin without any precipitating stress. Psychiatric disorders are defined by the sustained presence of specific signs (observable physical changes) or symptoms (subjective thoughts and feelings) that occur in predictable clusters called syndromes. These syndromes may clear within months, but there is a high probability that they will spontaneously recur with time.

There are several psychiatric disorders that may be triggered by stress. As many as 30% of family members may be diagnosed with disorders of major depression, anxiety, or substance abuse during the first two years of bereavement (Jacobs, 1993). These three disorders are commonly associated with bereavement and trauma, and present with persistent syndromes with signs and symptoms that distinguish them from the more common distress responses of trauma and separation. All three of these disorders may present in combination rather than isolation. These disorders are separable from retelling, but their coexistence may interfere with restoration. Depression may deepen the shadow of despair and self blame, anxiety may heighten the feeling of terror and disintegration, and substance abuse may thicken the veil of avoidance. One or a combination of these disorders creates an obstacle to restorative retelling and they are important to recognize and treat. Their treatment with specific medications or therapies helps, rather than interferes, with the retelling of the violent dying.

☐ **The Coherence of Resilience**

In the last chapter, I described resilience as a crucial mental capacity or reflex that maintained the level of experience within tolerable limits. Under normal circumstances you and I are not aware of its workings, but after an event that overwhelms the threshold for pain and personal safety we become aware of its absence. After Julie's suicide, the narrative dilemma of beginning and belonging in her story, the mandates from the public and private retellings, the intense waves of trauma and separation distress, and the mixture of possessive fantasies overwhelmed the limits of my mind. It was the return of my resilience that heralded my restorative retelling.

There were two innate attitudes that accompanied the return of my resilience. They can be best expressed in a simple, declarative mantra:

"I am safe and separate from what happens."

Obviously the sense of safety and separateness is beyond words (my nonverbal image of float and flow is more powerful to me), and not everyone shares equally in these resilient attitudes. Developmental psychologists have identified differences in resilience in human infants within hours of birth, and these differences are enduring. Some babies are not able to calm themselves when they are overstimulated. As they mature, they are less tolerant of overstimulation and insist on the proximity of their mother. They are born with a diminished capacity to calm or separate themselves when they experience internal or external stress, and this finding has been widely replicated in other studies of human infants and other primates. This strongly suggests that resilience is an intrinsic capacity with genetic transmission that persists into adulthood. Some individuals are not born with a robust resilience, and presumably are more vulnerable to overwhelming stress. Someone with this basic deficit may be unable to calm or separate from the disintegrating turbulence of intrusion and avoidance after the violent dying of someone he or she loved.

Mental health clinicians and epidemiologists have established that there is a strong association between diminished resilience and a developmental history of abuse and neglect. This suggests that the strength of resilience is also dependent upon its reinforcement. The constancy of nurturance and consistency from caregivers during critical periods of development is necessary for the maintenance of resilience. Some individuals are forced to live in families where abuse, neglect and disrespect erode the basis for safety and separateness. Those who have experienced repeated stress and trauma during their entire childhood might have never known resilience.

In addition to factors of nature and nurture, we recognize that resilience may be diminished by persistent stress. No matter how resilience was inherited or reinforced—it has limits. There may be enough resilience to begin a restorative retelling of violent dying, but additional stress may overcome the resilient "reserve." Additional stressors may come from any direction, but after a violent death they typically involve the withdrawal of support from family, work or the community. These resources may be absent or unavailable—or worse, they are available but resist involvement.

For example, family members might not want to listen to repeated retelling, or may become weary of cooperating with the efforts to make certain that they are safe. The family may turn disunited and distrustful. Fellow workers may grow impatient with persistent distractibility and continued absences—especially with an extended investigation and trial. The supervisor may insist that "you should be over this" and angry when he or she sees that productivity and performance goals have become trivialized by the tragedy. Friends no longer call to offer dinner invitations, or once at the table, they avoid talking about the dying.

The message seems the same from everyone: *"We are over this, and you should be too."*

Of course that's true—they have recovered. It's just as true that their insistence on a rapid recovery in someone who cannot, further drains their reserve of resilience.

They are weary of being resilient too. Yet their pushing or pulling the survivor away from what has happened is threatening rather than supportive. Their insistence on change leads to less, rather than more, resilience.

But how can a restorative retelling begin when resilience is being drained by the incoherence of violent dying and withdrawn by those who can no longer tolerate listening? In the next chapter, I introduce the stories of several family members who asked me for help and you will hear how I try to rediscover and reinforce resilience before the retelling begins. None of us can accommodate to the violent dying of someone we loved until and unless we find our own voice and person in what we retell. Being resilient, knowing that we are safe and separate, allows us to see and avoid the paradox of being ultimately responsible for a senseless dying.

Illustrations of Restorative Retelling

I have used my personal retelling of my wife's suicide as a basis for understanding the unfolding of a restorative retelling. The nonrestorative retelling needs to come from other voices. Understanding the basis for nonrestorative retelling begins with stories of family members who cannot remain resilient in the retelling. Each of these stories is based upon the personal retelling of a family member who presented for treatment and highlights a specific struggle in their incapacity to remain resilient while overwhelmed by possession or deadened by avoidance. Out of respect for their confidentiality, I have disguised their names and revised identifying features, but remained true to the dynamics of their story and their telling. I want you to listen with openness and an ear tuned for resilience instead of judgments or interpretations.

☐ Imaginary Retelling: Setting the Scene

Treating the highly distressed family member after a violent death draws me into an experience where no one belongs. I stand at the edge of an imaginary story of a tortured dying. Something unspeakably horrible has happened and a family member is beside me—facing the center of a scene that overwhelms.

At first there is nothing to be done and no one to be helped in that center. I belong at the periphery, and the priority is to keep the family member from disintegrating in the consuming story.

I offer a place of safety separate from the dying where the family member can regain their footing and orientation on the solid surface of living. Together we shield ourselves from directly considering or naming what has happened until the family member is calmer and is no longer drawn into the center of their imaginary terror.

A disciplined clinician can tolerate the unspeakable story without being terrorized or losing hope. The clinician's unperturbed presence begins a reassuring alliance so that naming and retelling the unspeakable can begin. There are theories that explain symptoms, verifiable diagnosis, effective medicines, and protocols of treatment, *but it is the calming alliance and the mutual retelling and revising of the dying story that is at the center of the work.*

The interplay between the family member and me is best illustrated by stories as they are retold during treatment. There are at least two semi-constant variables in these retellings. First, each story involves violent dying as the central drama, and second, I serve as the clarifier and narrator of the retelling. Of course, objectivity and constancy in these recountings is unattainable. In listening and retelling, my only constancy is my attitude of wonderment at what unfolds. I never know what to expect. Each story and teller and retelling is different than the last. In retelling there is a willingness to open and revise ourselves to the story we retell together. That degree of involvement in revising the story of a violent dying makes the work indelible. And not only for the family member. Each of these retellings revises my role as a clinician, and as a person. Allying with someone after a violent death is unforgettable.

To respect the absolute uniqueness of retelling, I follow the teller's lead. Restorative retelling requires an active attitude of creative searching and a high tolerance for ambiguity because it is so unpredictable. Insisting on a rigid protocol of retelling would diminish the teller's control in naming and choosing his or her own story.

Restoration is fundamentally uncertain because not only the story, but also the teller, is changed. The goal of restoration is to anticipate and encourage this change because the family member is rarely aware of his or her own transformation. Transformative change cannot begin if someone is rendered nonexistent in the retelling by terror or possession or witnessing. I serve as an ally for restorative change by attuning myself to the level of distress and orientation within the story and interrupt when distress becomes unbearable, or the teller and I become witnesses or possessions in the story rather than participants. I encourage participation in retelling the story to include a living memory and voice. Our living participation and presence in the retelling offers the choice to change our perspective.

While the path of restorative change is unpredictable, these illustrations of therapeutic retelling highlight restorative principles that I clarify and reinforce:

1. Therapeutic retelling begins by reestablishing resilience and moderating distress (to decrease distress when it overwhelms or to find when it is avoided),
2. Then revises (not relinquishes) the relationship with the dying and the deceased through restorative retelling,
3. And finally discovers a revitalized meaning and commitment in living.

☐ The Retelling of Avoidance

Maladaptive Avoidance: Valerie's Story

I met Valerie at The Washington State Correctional Center for Women. Since inmates have had multiple experiences with violent dying (many times higher than the general population), I volunteered to start a group therapy program for women prisoners.

Valerie signed up on the waiting list of women who wanted to attend. During our first visit she was so distressed that she timidly perched on the edge of the chair in her prison uniform (gray sweat shirt, gray sweat pants and white tennis shoes) and burst into tears. After composing herself, she said,

> *"Now that I'm not drugging, I can't keep myself from thinking and dreaming about my Mom and my boyfriend."*

Like almost every woman in prison, drugs and alcohol were a deeply embedded part of her life and crime. She had been addicted for many years and admitted that prison had probably saved her. She had an abiding faith in God, and she believed that her imprisonment was divinely directed—God was trying to save her by giving her a chance to change.

By 24, her life had been so chaotic that it was a wonder that she had survived. Her parents had been heroin addicts and her memories of her early childhood carried only traces of safety. Her attachment to her mother was vital, but it was reversed—she saw herself as responsible for her mother and her younger brother in protecting them from her abusive father. When she was 10, she witnessed the dying of both parents. Her father shot her mother in a drugged rage and then shot himself. The family and the life she recognized disintegrated in that moment of horror. She and her younger brother were placed in separate foster homes and she never saw him again. Within months she ran from any foster home or schoolroom to the streets, where she became addicted herself. Lost in the chaos of her fast life she would not allow herself to feel anything—including the loss of the custody of her two children. In the past 6 months she had witnessed the suicide of her long-term boyfriend that revived the memory of her mother's homicide. She tried to overdose with heroin to quiet the flash-backs and the sorrow that she had never allowed herself. A month before she was imprisoned, she armed herself and began robbing liquor stores.

Locked away from her abusive and self-destructive living, she wanted to examine and redirect her life. She was determined to attend classes to complete her G.E.D. and drug and alcohol treatment. Unfortunately, drug and alcohol treatment would not be available until her last month of incarceration. The Department of Corrections spends their limited treat-ment funds just before release when inmates are, in their estimation, most responsive. Valerie and I agreed that her addiction was so ingrained that she needed treatment for the full three years of her sentence if she was going to avoid relapsing.

That first visit with Valerie, as with most inmates, began in mutual frustration. We knew that she was in a time and space where she was protected from herself, that she was now realizing the emotional pain she had avoided (including her mother's homicide and her boyfriend's sui-cide) and that she wanted to change. Yet, the prison was more intent on correcting her misbehavior than treating her self-destructive motivation and addiction.

Starting a group therapy program in a prison is challenging. The ques-tions of trust and confidentiality are paramount in such a place, but Valerie was a spontaneous and open teller during the first session. Telling the story of her mother's homicide for the first time to a distrustful collection of convicts brought tears to everyone. I interrupted her telling several times to include us in her monologue so we could comfort her. Her will-ingness to divulge her vulnerability was soon modeled by the others, who now felt more committed to helping each other.

The group lasted for ten consecutive, weekly sessions of two hours each and followed an agenda that began with defining and reinforcing resil-ience, searching for internal strengths, and nurturing memories from the past. Those were hard for Valerie to find at first. However, by the fourth session she was the first member to give a commemorative presentation of the person who had died violently. Her boyfriend was twenty years older and had been more of a controlling father than boyfriend, but he had been kind to her. She rushed through this presentation to talk about her mother. With my encouragement, the group members kept a journal of their commemorative thoughts, and in writing about her mother she recalled her as a stable and warm figure who held her and combed her hair when she was small. It was as if she had uncovered a treasure, and she stroked her hair as she read her story of that comforting memory. Now she could recall that her mother hadn't used drugs or alcohol until she was six or seven, so there had been a long period of stability when she was smaller, "so there was a time when I was O.K."

In a later group she drew the scene of her mother's homicide. When I encouraged her to place herself in the drawing, she saw herself holding her mother and stroking her hair—telling her that she loved her before she went to heaven. It was an embracing farewell, and she recognized in the image and in herself that they had been close and would hold one another again after her own death. She began to appreciate that her self-destructive lifestyle was a shortcut to end her living so she could join her mother in death.

As the tenth session approached, there was great sadness and resistance to terminating. By this time Valerie had become one of the group leaders who was very caring and concerned about the other members—and had gained self-confidence from their appreciation and shared improvement. Her intrusive thoughts and dreams of the violent deaths had subsided. She could talk about those traumas without feeling that she was disintegrating and needed a fix. Now that she felt more stabilized and prepared to love and understand herself, she felt that a restorative change was beginning within her.

Comment: Violent dying seemed nearly inevitable in Valerie's chaotic childhood story. In her subsequent impulsive rush of self-destructive behavior, she had so little regard for herself that she could not view much purpose in life or living—beyond the moment of replacing pain with pleasure. Her chemical dependency seemed to be another inevitable way to protect her from feeling.

Ironically, prison offered a haven from the chaos she perpetuated for herself. By being contained and sober, Valerie was forced into a different perspective of herself and her future. She could no longer avoid who she was and who she would become. Without avoidance and drug abuse, she wanted to change herself and the direction of her life.

The time-limited group gave her an opportunity to retell the homicide of her mother, and for the first time to put words and feelings to what she had witnessed. In commemorating her mother, she found a reservoir of forgotten memories of warmth and security that had been lost in her avoidance of the memory of her mother's homicide. That nurturing memory was restorative. Knowing that she had been loved allowed her to remember her mother in a context of value and security beyond the violent dying.

I last met Valerie in the prison courtyard. I was walking to the clinic to lead a newly formed group and she was on her way to school. She smiled as she told me that she was feeling stronger and more hopeful and encouraged me to keep leading groups. There is a long waiting list, and Valerie has actively recruited and referred several members.

It was good to see her, but the same, unspoken frustration clouded that meeting, as it had our first—that she was ready for more help than prison would offer. She will leave after she serves her time instead of using her time to serve a change in herself.

Avoidance as Adaptive: Charles and Barbara's Story

Charles, a seventeen year-old youngster, came to see me at his mother's insistence. His older brother, Herb, had committed suicide four months before and Charles had carried on his normal routine as if nothing had happened. They were apparently as close as two brothers could be. That made Herb's suicide even more traumatic. No one suspected that Herb was depressed or plotting his death until he was found hanging in his college dormitory room with a suicide note pinned to his chest. Charles rarely mentioned Herb, refused to visit his grave with his parents, and explained that he had made his own peace with Herb's death. He was willing to come to reassure his mother, Barbara, but didn't think that he needed help.

After visiting with Charles and his parents I suspected that I was serving as a psychiatric authority to reassure his parents that he was safe. Charles and I agreed that he was, and I also presumed that Charles felt threatened in being identified as potentially suicidal. He had been so closely identified with Herb that he needed some distance from the way he had died. We reviewed what they might expect in their adjustment as a family and they agreed to consult with me again in several months—or sooner if there was any difficulty.

Six months later Charles' mother again requested a consultation. Charles seemed all right and was focused more on the future than his past. He had decided to attend a small college on the East Coast and was looking forward to the transition.

He thought about Herb often, and mostly of their good times together. Herb's decision to kill himself remained an unanswered puzzle. After several weeks of agonizing inquiry, Charles chose to *"remember Herb the way he would want to be remembered."* He was not preoccupied with imaginary reenactments of the dying or possessive thoughts of remorse or self-doubt. There had been several dreams that felt restorative. In each dream he greeted Herb who reassured him that he was safe, but sad that he was alone. In the last dream Charles told Herb of his acceptance at college. Herb smiled and congratulated him as they embraced and said goodbye.

He denied any signs or symptoms of disabling distress or psychiatric disorder, and emphasized that he was not, and never had been, suicidal. Though he recognized that Herb's suicide would always be surrounded with sadness and uncertainty, he did not anticipate that it would greatly influence his own living.

Charles was concerned about his mother. She couldn't accept that he was going to be safe. Her constant checking and monitoring of where and how he was, was understandable, but burdensome. He recognized that his departure for college was going to be very distressing for her.

I asked to see Charles' mother, Barbara, by herself, and they smiled nervously at one another as they passed in my doorway. She was so determined to remain strong for Charles that I didn't want our interview to risk humiliating her. I suspected that she was struggling to maintain control, and I wanted privacy for her as she told me her own story of Herb's dying.

I began by trying to reassure her.

> *"Barbara, I am confident that Charles is going to be O.K. But this must be overwhelming for you as his mother—to have to be so strong for him while dealing with your own grief. Tell me, what's it been like for you?"*

Within minutes she began to cry as she told her own story and admitted that she needed help. For the last two months she had been depressed and could not stop blaming herself for Herb's suicide, which she witnessed every day in her thoughts and dreams. I told her that I was not surprised—that most parents went through a very painful time after the suicide of their child, and she deserved an opportunity to retell someone the story she couldn't stop telling herself. I was confident that she would be less distressed when she allowed someone else to help her through this tragedy. I also supported her avoidance in sharing too much of her own distress with Charles and her husband until she was more comfortable with her own retelling.

I suggested that she return to see one of my associates, not because I was hesitant in becoming her therapist, but because I wanted to remain available for Charles for the next year or two. I didn't anticipate that he would need help, but it might become complex if they both needed me at the same time. I didn't want to place myself between them, as a shared therapist and listener, unless the three of us were meeting together to retell the same story. I knew that her retelling was very different than Charles', and that she needed her own private opportunity to come to terms with her own distress and possessions. However, I emphasized that I remained available for a family session if that would be of support for her. Since the family interactions were solid and supportive at this point, there was no urgency.

It has been nearly ten years since I saw Charles, who is now an attorney on the East Coast. As he predicted, he hasn't needed any clinical help. He devotes some of his practice to pro bono service for families that need legal assistance after a violent death. His mother made substantial progress in treatment with my associate that lasted for nearly a year. She was treated with an antidepressant for her major depressive disorder, as well as individual therapy, and then joined a time-limited support group for family members after a violent dying. She has also served as a volunteer and leader of a peer support group for parents of children who committed suicide. The combination of medication and focused therapy, followed by her helping others, was restorative.

Comment: My role with Charles in retelling the story of his brother's suicide was more of observer than ally. Within several months of the suicide, his distress was not preoccupying, and he could remember his brother's living more than his dying. His resilience was quickly reestablished with little evidence of reenactment, remorse, or self-doubt. Charles did not actively deny or disavow the long-term impact of Herb's suicide, yet was confident that he could accommodate himself to those changes without clinical intervention. Time has shown his own prognosis to be accurate, and, like most family members after a violent dying, his self-generated accommodation has been durable.

My role with his mother was more active and intervening. Her intense distress over Herb's suicide was reflected in an insistence that Charles receive the support and treatment that she wouldn't seek for herself. Her fear for his safety was, in part, a way of avoiding her own fear of her own disintegration. While Charles' avoidance of therapy was adaptive, Barbara's initial avoidance of therapy for herself was maladaptive. As she felt more stable through her own restorative retelling, she could see that Charles was going to survive as well. Gradually, as she regained a confidence in her own living, she was able to reengage with Charles as a concerned parent—rather than a hovering mother obsessed with fears of imminent dying.

☐ The Retelling of Possession

Reenactment: Robert's Story

I could see that Robert was frightened as we shook hands in the waiting room before our first visit. As we sat down in my office, I reassured him that I recognized how difficult this was for him. I knew that his wife had died four years before, and we would talk about that at some point, but first I wanted to know what his life had been like before her death.

He looked startled, not expecting that sort of question, *"My life ended when my wife and baby were killed,"* he said. Then he began to talk about himself when he had felt alive.

He had enjoyed an unusually privileged life in a prestigious East Coast family. His childhood memories were happy to recollect. He had gone to a private boarding school and an Ivy League college before joining a brokerage firm in New York. His life seemed to coast from one secure haven to another. Moving to Seattle had been one of the few things he had dared. He loved mountain climbing and sailing, and Seattle offered a novelty his life had lacked.

His involvement with Debbie was unexpected. She was working as a checker where he shopped for groceries. They were so unmatched that they often wondered how their relationship started.

Over the next several sessions we reviewed picture albums that memorialized their mutual joy in shaping one another—she to his sophistication and he to her social innocence. Most of the pictures were of their sailing trips and mountain hikes. Their devotion grew and when she accepted his marriage proposal she finally told him of her flight from her first husband and his psychotic threats to kill her. But he was back on the East Coast. He could never trail her. They told each other they would be safe in Seattle.

They had been married for less than a year, and she was pregnant with their child, when her first husband stalked and killed her and then killed himself.

Robert's living seemed to partially dissolve in her dying. He hadn't been able to sail or work in four years. He kept his boat on shore and stopped hiking. He drove a taxi at night because the flashbacks of her dying would wake him. He admitted that some part of him wanted to continue living—he hadn't sold his boat and he still followed the stock market and handled his own investments—but he was living at half speed. I encouraged him to begin working on the boat and he agreed that he needed to recapture some momentum in his life.

Now that he was more stable, we agreed to talk more directly about Debbie's dying. It was always in his thoughts. He was still having terrifying flashbacks and dreams of her murder. We agreed that since he had never told the full story, he or I could interrupt it at any point if it became too painful. It came with a rush, but he was able to finish without stopping or leaving the room despite his tears of despair and anger and remorse.

That session was pivotal. He and I knew that he could survive what had happened, now that he had given it words and we had a story to retell. After this session, the flashbacks and the dreams of her dying were less intense, but persisted, and we agreed that it was difficult to name the dynamic action of his imaginary story. At my urging he drew out his image of the dying on a large sheet of paper with colored pencils. I still have the drawing, a series of dreadful scenes, not only depicting the brutality of her killing, but his fantasy of what she was thinking and feeling as she was dying:

"Robert, where are you—it hurts so bad—oh my baby!!"

I told him how horrified I felt in seeing what he had been replaying before himself for four years, and noted that he was nowhere in the drawing:

"You aren't in the drawing—because you weren't there—but in your imagination you must be, because you keep telling yourself this same story. Show me where you would put yourself if you could have been there."

He immediately placed himself between Debbie and her killer, where he grabbed the gun and killed him. Then he held Debbie and calmed her. Then he began crying as he recognized that he had never said goodbye to her—and he did.

We looked at those drawings only once, and he insisted on leaving them with me. I saw Robert for a single follow-up session. He felt confident that he could manage on his own.

I still get Christmas cards—a picture of his new wife and child—and from a distance we can share what we started with our restorative retelling. I still have the drawings of Debbie's dying. They represent the reality of what he and I could retell, but not deny. He left that picture of her dying filed away with his therapy notes, and away from his living.

Comment: Robert's living had been enriching and consistent before the murder of his wife and baby. Debbie's death had suddenly untracked his very stable view of himself and the future. Afterward, he was emptied of meaning and initiative by haunting images of her agony as she was dying. When we had prepared ourselves a stable and safe place, we opened ourselves to what had happened through words and drawings. In the story of her dying, he found a role that he had lost—her loving protector. It did not take him long to reclaim that identity, and that was the basis for a restorative narrative and a reconnection with his living.

Remorse: Pat's Story

Pat and I became discouraged in retelling her son's dying in a car accident. It brought little relief despite our meeting once a week for over a year. Since his death she felt a failure at most things she tried, including therapy.

Pat's 19-year-old son drove off a mountain road as he was returning to college after the Christmas break. His pancreas was ruptured and he died within a week, despite the heroic efforts of teams of doctors and repeated surgeries. Pat could not stop her fantasies of how he had been injured as the car tumbled off the mountain road, and could not tolerate her memories of his last days of suffering in the hospital. She was inconsolable because she blamed herself for his death. Her son had always been somewhat passive and dependent upon her. They were inseparable, and though he was away at college, she continued to talk with him on the phone each day. She constructed a web of self-recriminations around his accident—she should have kept him from driving "because it was snowing"; she should have insisted that he drive her car "because it has air bags"; she should have insisted that he be transferred to another hospital "because they do pancreatic transplants." There was an endless list of alternatives she "should have" considered that would have avoided his dying. For three years she continued to visit the gravesite each day to leave fresh flowers and continue conversing with him, unable to accept that he was "gone." Her husband and younger son could neither share her remorse nor understand her resistance in separating from the gravesite. One night her dead son appeared at the foot of her bed and wordlessly bid her to join him in death. That frightened her. She welcomed death and their reunion, but she couldn't leave her younger son and husband. For their sake, she called and asked for help.

There was no question that she also had a recurrent, major depressive disorder, which had required treatment several years before. Since she had responded to medication, I restarted her on the same antidepressant. That cleared her symptoms of low energy and initiative as well as her insomnia and loss of appetite, but it didn't touch her remorse or her adherent vigil at her son's grave.

Despite our hours of retelling his childhood and her nurturing role as his mother, Pat continued to punish herself for his dying. She would stand at his graveside each day and cry out for his forgiveness. She felt enraged at God and had not felt any solace or comfort from her minister. Church now felt like an empty, meaningless gathering. She refused to consider my suggestion that her faith might return with time, nor could we interrupt her compulsion to visit his grave that restricted her radius between home and the cemetery because she had to place fresh flowers on his grave each day.

We included her family in our retelling. Her husband and surviving son were supportive of her therapy and were puzzled by her fixation on the accident. There had been other deaths in her primary family in recent years that had not undermined her. There was nothing detectable from her past that would predict that she would be so vulnerable.

Her self-blaming distress was centered on her imaginary vigil over his bed as he was dying from his ruptured pancreas. She never left his room for the week that he was in the hospital, and never admitted that he might not survive. He wept and tried to talk about his fear of dying, but she remained stoic and denying.

During one particularly quiet session, I found myself imagining that Pat and I were at her son's bedside together, sharing her lonely vigil. I wondered out loud how we might ask her son for help in resolving our dilemma. Maybe he would have some advice for us that would help her. I asked her to write an imaginary letter, from her son, to tell us how we could help his mother. This was the letter that she brought to the next session:

> *Dear Mom and Dr. Rynearson,*
>
> *I will try to help you. Mom, you know that I don't want you to stay so sad and hopeless and I don't think it's good for you to visit my grave so often. You've got to start living more for you and the family and start taking better care of yourself.*
>
> *Don't give up on my Mom, Dr. Rynearson, she's real stubborn and she won't give up, so don't you.*
>
> *I want you to be happy again, Mom. Remember what I wrote on the first Mother's Day card I made for you:*
>
> > *I love my Mom*
> > *Because she dances*
> > *And sings around the house*
> > *And reads me stories and poems*
> > *And smiles at me with her eyes*
> > > *Love, David*

This was the first in a series of letters she wrote herself through her son that began to ease her remorse. It was as if she was able to forgive herself through him.

Several months later, she was relieved to hold her grandson minutes after his birth—he was named David, after her dead son—and his replacing presence and her caring for him was a tangible way to retell his living. In watching him grow and being his grandmother, she recaptured some meaning and purpose for herself, and her faith in God was rekindled as she attended his baptism. However, she continues the vigilant attendance at her son's grave.

Comment: Our retelling the story of her son's dying didn't release her from the self-imposed relationship of blaming and shame she continued at his graveside. Treatment of her clinical depression resolved the physical signs and symptoms of her depressive disorder, but had little influence on her trauma distress and separation distress or her remorseful possession.

Pat felt some relief in the forgiveness that she was able to project through her imaginary writings from her deceased son, but it was the birth of her grandson and her enactment of protective nurturance with him that returned her sense of identity and meaning. Her attachment to her son's graveside is less intense and compulsive—she must take him fresh flowers every week or two—but now she mourns his absence, rather than begging for his forgiveness.

Retaliation: Ralph's Story

Ralph's teenage daughter had been brutally raped and beaten to death by an unknown assailant two years before. Ralph was devoted to his children, though he was separated from them at the time of her death. He and his wife had divorced the week before his daughter ran away from home and was killed while hitchhiking. Ralph moved back with his former wife and remaining children and began a relentless search for his daughter's assailant. He rearranged his work schedule so he would be available during the day to attend briefings with his lawyer and the police and hired his own private detective and began his own investigation while accumulating his own evidence and systematic records. After several months, he and the local police were in agreement that a prime suspect was probably responsible for her killing, but the police did not believe that the case was strong enough to warrant his arrest. For the next year, Ralph continued to follow this suspect, and when he learned that he was moving to another state, Ralph became more deliberate about directly retaliating or hiring a killer. His ex-wife, suspecting his plans, confronted him. He grimly agreed to see a therapist, though he denied any distress beyond frustrated revenge.

Ralph was not a willing participant in psychotherapy, and I was hesitant in committing myself as his therapist. It was difficult for us to begin treatment when he felt little motivation for change or cooperation. Before treatment began, I reminded him that I would not collude in his murder plans and that I had an ethical and legal obligation to report my concern that he might retaliate.

He didn't want to create more catastrophes. He recognized that if he was involved in more violent death, he risked more traumas for everyone he loved. There was enough concern for him and his family that he chose to give up his plans for retaliation while seeing me for several sessions—to see where it would lead.

He wanted to talk about the dying as if it were an unsolved crime that he had solved. I listened for several minutes and interrupted,

> *"Ralph, we aren't going to discover what I want to know about your daughter by just talking about her dying. I don't know anything about her as a person—you haven't even called her by name. What was her name?"*

Her name was Chris, and naming her brought her closer. So did the album of pictures that showed her in his arms as the youngest of his three children and his only daughter, and always at his side as she grew older. In many of the pictures she was holding his hand, and gazing up at him. I wondered if that represented something in their relationship.

He began to cry as he remembered their attachment. That bond had been strong from the beginning and strengthened by the days and nights when her asthma would worsen. He was the parent who was responsible for her medicines and inhaler—and would take her to the emergency room when she could barely breathe. Those were frightening times, but they were confident that he could calm and attend to her until she could breathe again.

Their attachment was interrupted by his decision to divorce and move out.

The entire family was in turmoil over Chris's stormy adolescence and drug abuse that had started several years before. Ralph and his wife decided to divorce because it seemed that they had nothing left for each other—and if they had separate homes, they could at least share in trying to manage Chris. Now he felt that his leaving was a mistake.

This history was gathered in our first six sessions and Ralph began to appreciate that there was more to this than retaliation. Now he began to have a recurring nightmare of her dying. He could not remember the specifics of the dream—only that he would awake feeling breathless and terrified. He agreed to keep pen and paper at his bedside so he could draw the dream and write down the details if it awakened him again.

It did, and he brought the drawing of the dream to our session so we could retell it together. In the crude drawing there were two struggling stick figures in the center—one lying on top of the other—and above both figures was a unicorn flying toward an apparent sunrise. I could not see Ralph in the drawing. He said that he was the figure that was being raped and killed. The unicorn was Chris. That had been her favorite mythical beast and in the dream she was released from the rape and violent death, while he took her place to protect her from the terror and dying— and her smothering.

After ten more sessions of treatment, the dreams had stopped and he felt less intense over retaliating. In those sessions he could be more accepting of his own guilt in abandoning Chris and his family when they had needed him the most. He no longer threatened a personal vendetta against her murderer.

Ralph called me a year later to report that Chris's murderer was now in prison and he and his ex-wife wanted the name of a marriage counselor. They were still living together with the children and were considering remarrying. He wasn't enthused about more therapy, but he was willing to see someone for a few sessions if it would help.

Comment: Ralph's repressed vulnerability and guilt after his daughter's murder was connected with his active plan to kill the killer. Talking about his daughter as a person whose life he treasured, rather than a moral transgression that he needed to avenge, brought back his role as father.

He was not motivated for treatment. His treatment was brief and supportive because he was not comfortable with ambiguity. His awareness of his repressed remorse and grief in her murder somehow diminished his need to retaliate.

Protection: Maggie's Story

The therapist who referred Maggie to me was concerned that she would not attend the interview without her family. Maggie was so frightened of leaving home that she would only agree to an appointment if she could bring her daughter and her mother with her. I assured the therapist that I wanted to meet with all of them during the first visit.

Maggie and her mother and daughter stood as one when I introduced myself. Maggie was in the midst of a panic attack and looked stricken, while her mother and daughter looked to me with a combination of desperation and relief. Maggie was sure she was having a heart attack. I reassured her it was more probably an anxiety attack related to leaving home and seeing me, and I invited all three of them into my office so we could sort things out together. She was hyperventilating and her pulse was strong and steady, but rapid. She calmed considerably in knowing that she would not be alone. She did not want me to ask her a lot of questions. I told her:

"This is not the time for me to ask you questions. This is a time we have to help you find some way to feel safe."

We spent the next hour in family consultation trying to establish where and how we might help Maggie feel protected. All three of them dreaded returning to their house that had been transformed into a death scene after watching Maggie's son being murdered on the front porch a month before. Maggie's older sister had urged them to move in with her until they could begin looking for another place. We called her from my office, and it was decided that they would go there that afternoon. Maggie agreed to start on a low dose of an anti-anxiety medication to control her panic attacks and insomnia and we would meet after the weekend. We all agreed that it was mandatory that her daughter return to school, and arranged to have one of her school mates escort her to and from her aunt's house so Maggie knew she was not alone. As they left, I called the employee assistance worker at Maggie's company and endorsed a medical leave of absence for at least a month.

At our next meeting, Maggie and her mother attended without the daughter. Maggie was markedly improved with the combination of the move and the physical effect of the medication. Without the panic, she had slept for the first time since her son's murder and was beginning to feel less disintegrated. She no longer felt a pervasive dread of immanent death and could appreciate that she and her daughter could survive what had happened. She not only brought in pictures of her son, but also of her husband, and over the next several weeks we commemorated both of their lives.

She and her husband had traveled from Texas to Seattle ten years before to find decent jobs. They both worked on the production line at Boeing while her mother watched the children during the day. Maggie's husband died unexpectedly from a heart attack, and life and order seemed to rush out of the family with his death. Her children were teenagers and her son, Harry, began to run unbridled with a gang. Maggie and her daughter and mother witnessed his death in a drive-by shooting on their front porch. Now they were terrified. Maggie felt alone and vulnerable without her husband and son.

Maggie's life in her primary family and with her husband and children had been stable and supportive. There was a definite history of anxiety disorder in the women in her family—Maggie's mother and two of her three sisters had been treated for panic—so there was an acceptance of that problem as a disorder that needed medication.

At the end of that first month of therapy Maggie was no longer taking medication. She purchased a new home closer to her daughter's school, which diminished her protective concern, and now that her daughter was back in school full time, Maggie felt ready to return to work. Her return to her church for Sunday services and prayer meetings during the week brought back her faith that her son was at peace with his father, *"and they're waiting for me there."*

I continued to see her for counseling for another ten sessions and at my urging we focused on her husband's death rather than her son's murder. We knew that her relationship with her husband had been foundational and I wanted to summon that relationship as a source of stabilizing memories before focusing on her son's violent dying.

She felt relieved by retelling a restorative narrative of her husband, and now that she was back at work full time, her self-confidence had returned. She decided against further treatment. By that time, the trial for her son's murder was finished and with the support of her church and her surviving family she would be all right. I agreed, but with the provision that she call if her panic recurred or she began to retell her son's murder with overwhelming reenactment or remorse.

Maggie and her mother and daughter and I met for her last session, as we had for her first. Now she led them into my office. They were satisfied that Maggie could manage. She was still overprotective with her daughter and we agreed that she probably would remain so. I emphasized to the mother and the daughter that now that Maggie was stabilized, it might be their turn to receive some help in their adjustment, and not to hesitate in calling for assistance or referral. I haven't heard from any of them since that visit.

Comment: Maggie was so traumatized after witnessing her son's homicide that she exhausted herself and her mother and daughter with her frantic overprotectiveness. Violent dying was an external preoccupation more than an internal memory and she felt more distress for her daughter's safety than her own traumatic despair.

Engaging someone this terrorized demands direct measures to moderate distress by reinforcing their sense of safety—a secure home, assurance that they and surviving family members are protected and financially secure. Once Maggie and the family she gathered around her began trusting that they were not in danger of being attacked, Maggie was able to gather herself from within. Her panic cleared with a short course of medication and, feeling more resilient, she found further stability in returning to work and to her church.

Because of the intensity of her terror and her incapacity to calm herself, I urged her to retell the commemorative story of her husband to divert her from the horror of her son's killing. Of course there were references to her son's living memory as she talked about her husband, but these were experiences that she celebrated as well. We delayed directly considering the homicide until she chose to retell it herself. The trial of her son's murderers stirred her reenactment thoughts and overprotective compulsions, but she was not overwhelmed.

She and her family were satisfied with her progress and with her decision to terminate treatment. I respected her decision to avoid retelling her son's violent dying. I suspect that witnessing his killing was so unspeakably horrible for Maggie that it was better left unsaid. She and I settled for her indirect revision of that violent dying by retelling the more coherent story of her relationship with her husband and son before their deaths. That is a story she can live with.

☐ Summary

These personalized retellings convey the active attitude of wonderment and improvisation that underlies restorative retelling. In my role as a clinician, I participate in the unique retelling of violent dying with the restorative goal of reconnecting living memories and experience beyond the event of the dying. This active searching for living, within the traumatic telling of dying, twists and turns in the retelling of experiences we summon together.

The image of water and its connection with forces that we cannot see helps in my clinical work. Like being in a small boat far from shore with only our retelling to guide us, I can't know or predict precisely where we are, but I am aware of forces and points of reference that will carry us in a restorative direction: The level of distress is the first referent, and I am like a helmsman at the tiller, attuned to the direction and level of the surrounding energy. Like wind and current; distress is invisible—but I can sense its effects. Too much distress and we are swept away by the telling, with no distress we are becalmed. We master distress by sensing its direction and force, and piloting ourselves within its flow.

Our alignment to the memory of the deceased, their dying and their living, is the second referent. Like a navigator, I pause to make soundings and sightings during the retelling to plot our position. The path of our retelling depends on our orientation to that memory and the willingness to press on, or circle, or turn around.

Our pursuit of meaning is the third referent, and like a captain, I assume responsibility for guiding our retelling towards a harbor of refuge. I give reassurance that by retelling, we can remain afloat until we anchor and disembark. Our goal is to arrive and reengage with living on shore, and once there, we are expected to steer, navigate and captain ourselves.

What sort of landing have we found in these retellings?

Valerie knows that prison offers a refuge from her life on the streets, but it is not in a place that she welcomes or wants. Unfortunately, prison cannot offer the extensive rehabilitation that would help her. Now that she is sober and has renewed her faith in God, she has rediscovered a fragile, loving memory of her mother that brings self-worth and the hope that she can change and survive for herself. Her own life and future are beginning to matter to her.

Charles and Barbara found some of their restorative meaning connected to Herb's suicide by choosing to help others who struggle with the effects of violent dying—Charles as an attorney and Barbara as a support group leader.

Robert found meaning through his reconnection with work and beginning a new family that gave him another chance to be a husband and father.

Pat rediscovered some reconnection with her warmth as a mother through her imaginary communication with David. The birth of her grandson gave her nurturance a tangible purpose and direction.

As Ralph surrendered his role as retaliator, he renewed his commitment to his ex-wife and children. By restoring his marriage and family, he found a sense of permanence and consistency beyond himself and Chris's death.

Maggie's restoration began by removing herself from the scene of her son's homicide. Buoyed by her belief in the peaceful afterlife she would share with her dead son and husband, she returned to work. An increasing confidence in her own safety returned value and hope to her living.

Retelling the violent dying and living of someone in their family restored these people. In each retelling, like a successful sailing, we first reconstructed a resilient deck on which to work and rest, then a confidence that we could find and master currents and winds, then a reorienting remembrance of the shore behind us that would guide us to a place that would be different because it would be new, and we would be changed.

5
CHAPTER

Restorative Retelling for Kids

Sitting across from Valerie in the prison clinic as she first recounted her mother being killed by her father, and then killing himself, was traumatic. As she began that retelling, we were transported backwards into the time and space of her experience as a terrorized ten-year-old child. Because of her imprisonment and enforced sobriety, this was the first time she had allowed herself to tell the story to someone else, and like her, I was struggling to avoid her horror and helplessness.

No matter how many times I am the first listener for the first telling, I feel avoidant and overwhelmed because I know where the action will carry us. Like the teller, I anticipate the release of uncontrolled terror. However, once Valerie began to cry, I could gain some distance from her feelings by actively comforting her and reassuring her that it was safe to feel this way—that we would survive this story together. Of course, by being a reassuring listener I placed myself in a role that Valerie and many other children who experience violent dying have never shared: They had no caring adult to reassure that they were safe and separate enough from the memory of the violent dying that they could retell it. Without an opportunity to retell their memory of violent dying the child may carry that experience within, as stark and raw as the moment that it happened. Valerie could not forget, and like every child who survives trauma and cannot retell it, her mother's violent dying was a repetitive theme in her own living. Her mother's murder was so buried and secret that her way of retelling the tragedy was to act it out—to become a dramatic character in her own destruction so she would kill or be killed. When Valerie was finally confined in prison, sober and safe from her self-destruction, she could begin to acknowledge what had happened and to feel safe and comforted. I wish that I, or some responsible adult, could have been there when she was ten when we could have begun a restorative retelling together. That opportunity may have given her enough autonomy from that awful memory that her living would have felt more hopeful and meaningful.

☐ Imaginary Accommodation

The way that children cope with violent death has been foundational to my understanding of restorative retelling. I have great respect for the inclusiveness of their inner life. Professionally and personally, I have sometimes found guidance in their ways of thinking and feeling. Adult awareness is less vivid and immediate. When we were children, our view of our self and our world was more direct and unreflective. We shared an open wonderment and inventiveness in understanding what occurred around or within us. Awareness was more spontaneous and connected with imagination.

In an imaginary world, thoughts and feelings and behaviors are unfettered by logic or barriers of time or space. Everything is possible and nothing is improbable. Imagination mixes and merges living and death. You may remember the story that my four-year-old daughter told me within the first several weeks of Julie's suicide. It was a vivid reversal of her dying. Julie was "playing a game" with us by disappearing, but now she missed us and would come home soon. In telling and retelling the story with me we shared transcendence from what had happened. Her story softened the dying memory within a context of timelessness and suspension so she could begin to "realize" what she couldn't understand or accept—that Julie had suddenly left, and would never return. The words and the plot of her story allowed us to wordlessly accept how much we missed her and would never forget her. Retelling her magical story of return helped us regain a sense of control over our traumatic separation from Julie, and remember her warmth and concern for us. It was better that I remained quiet and reflective at the telling of her story and didn't interrupt with my rational questioning. Later I recognized how natural and reparative her imaginary story could be for me—not because Julie would magically come back, but because I could be enlivened in my memory of her vitality before she died.

After a violent death, a child invariably imagines how the death could be reversed, and for the very small child, whoever died is still alive and needs to be rescued. To view children as childish and this thinking as wasteful would be a mistake. While these imaginary beliefs of permanence and return from dying are wishful, they are also restorative and necessary for the child, as well as adults, when they first begin to retell the story of violent dying. Imaginary stories of reunion, rescue, and reversal are purposeful myths that restore us from our immersion in violent dying. They offer a narrative connection with living instead of disintegrating in the narrative of dying and death. Many children and adults retell such stories for a time. These stories do not need to be challenged unless and until they persist and assume a mythic reality that interferes with reengagement with others.

For some adults and children who cannot stop themselves from retelling the reenactment of the dying, these purposeful, revitalizing myths can be encouraged as a first step in restorative retelling. When an adult is possessed with imaginary reenactment I encourage him or her to become more childlike and to draw his or her imaginary stories of reenactment and restoration that we retell between us. As a nonverbal communication, drawings convey a more immediate and incisive imagery of restoration than the "too many" words of description that usually draw us further from the imaginary experience. I consider this exercise of imaginary commemoration and death imagery as progressive and healthful rather than an immature, childish regression.

☐ Maladaptive Responses

It is not surprising that children are at risk for maladaptive responses to violent dying. They may develop intense reenactment imagery or secondary possessions of remorse, overprotectiveness or retaliation and comorbid disorders of anxiety, depression, or substance abuse. The effects of the violent dying are long-lasting and are reprocessed as children and adolescents continue to accommodate to subsequent experiences of trauma, and separation and attachment. While younger family members may develop age-specific responses to violent dying, there are more similarities than differences between adults and children in adjusting to a violent death.

Children and adolescents carry the same risk factors that have been documented in adults—individual factors such as sex (girls are more distressed), age (preschoolers are most vulnerable), previous history of abuse or comorbid psychiatric disorder and characteristics of the violent dying (actual witnessing is most traumatic), and relationship with the deceased (close emotional relationship) are all associated with increased distress.

Age-specific differences in children after the violent death of a family member are dependent upon the relative immaturity of their cognitive and emotional responses. Small children not only magically assume that a violent death may be reversed, but may magically assume that they are somehow responsible for what happened. That dreadful compensatory story, *They Died Because I Did Something Wrong*, carries so much guilt that it needs to be interrupted. Although it provides the child with an aberrant sense of control over the dying, it does not point in a restorative direction. Children are relieved to know that this mythic story of remorse can be retold with a different ending—that many of us feel guilty after the violent death of someone we love, but whoever died probably wouldn't blame us for what happened, and we need to forgive ourselves too.

School age children are usually less communicative. Their avoidance of the emotional impact of the violent dying is a reflection of an apparent latency in their neuropsychological responses. Between the ages of six and the advent of adolescence, many children seem less perturbed by experiences of trauma and separation, including violent dying. Dying is something that might pervade their play or their favorite television show or video game, but is not given voice. This is an age when girls and boys are more preoccupied with maintaining close relationships with their best friends and engaging in new found activities than sharing private distresses and doubts. This does not mean that the violent dying of a family member hasn't had a profound impact, but the impact registers as a latent or unexpressed memory.

With adolescence comes the capacity to consider dying and death in its stark and inevitable formlessness—and a growing acceptance of personal mortality. The emotional responses to dying and death are no longer so latent or avoided. Adolescence is a time when the permanence of relationships may be particularly important, and the loss of a parent or sibling or a best friend to a violent death may be very destabilizing. The relationship with the deceased may have been highly charged and cannot be magically replaced or stoically avoided. The effects of reenactment and possession are more powerful at this age, and may be impulsively acted out rather than held and retold. Enactments may include compulsive avoidance (e.g., substance abuse, sexual acting out, eating or spending binges, risk-taking to defy death) or more direct expression of retaliation (e.g., homicidal reprisal—particularly in adolescent boys) or remorse (e.g., suicidal reprisal).

☐ Interventions for Children and Adolescents

There are two categories of intervention for children after a violent death that are designed (1) to meet their acute need for support immediately after the event, and (2) to provide a longer-term therapy to help them in accommodating to trauma and separation distress.

Emotional "debriefing" has become a popular, acute intervention for children. It is commonly promoted by school administrators and counselors to help children in immediately processing their responses to the violent death of a schoolmate. Debriefings encourage an open classroom discussion of the event to explore the children's' thoughts and feelings, clarify misconceptions about the dying, identify coping strategies, and promote support from others. Finally, such debriefings also help identify and refer at-risk children for assessment and possible treatment.

Despite the widespread use of classroom debriefing, there is no research documenting its effectiveness, its benefits or its most appropriate timing. It seems that administrators, counselors, and parents are so intent on actively responding to the crisis of a violent death, that they collectively intervene without knowing which children need support and how that might be accomplished. Instead, everyone is drawn into the same net. Debriefing has become such a popular trend that it cannot await an objective review of its utility. Despite its untested and collective use, debriefing probably helps in identifying some vulnerable kids who need more detailed assessment and treatment. There are, however, very few communities that offer specialized services for children and adolescents highly distressed by violent death. Those who promote acute debriefing interventions for kids rarely ensure that there are existent local services before acting on their well-intentioned effort to support children and adolescents by challenging their avoidance. Some vulnerable kids may be unprepared to handle the open discussion of thoughts and feelings that debriefing encourages.

Clinicians who work with children in individual treatment after a violent death have the requisite time and setting to develop a deeper understanding of coping mechanisms and the pattern of responses, including dreams and fantasies. Since children can be more expressive through their drawings and play, child therapists are skilled and familiar in interpreting what children are projecting about themselves in their art and playful dramas. Treatments with children naturally deal with retelling and include goals of moderating distress and revising the relationship with the deceased as the dying story is modified.

Most child therapists have at some time in their career treated children and adolescents after a violent death with a form of supportive, individual treatment. There are a few anecdotal reports of these treatments, but there has been no systematic outcome study of children or adolescents treated with an intervention specific for the maladaptive effects of violent dying. It is discouraging that individual treatment after violent dying, the most common intervention for kids as well as adults, has been so sparsely studied, despite the many thousands of children who have presumably been helped.

On their own, children are less likely to seek assistance. It is rare for a child or adolescent to recognize his or her reactions to a violent death as maladaptive, or to turn to someone outside the immediate family or circle of friends to help them through this personal tragedy. A concerned adult— a parent, an older sibling, a grandparent, or caring extended family member—brings most youngsters to the office of a clinician or a peer-led support group leader. They have noticed some change in this young family member that warrants attention. The changes may be specific to the violent dying (e.g., phobic behaviors, insomnia and nightmares, fears of safety, and insistence on proximity) or non-specific (e.g., diminished attention and energy, school failure, irritability, or social isolation). Rarely, as with Barbara and her son Charles, the adult may be indirectly asking for attention for their his or her distress. A responsible adult who needs to be actively included initiates intervention. Regardless of the sort of intervention, it is the responsible adult who brings the youngster to sessions and reinforces the importance of continuing. These adults need to know that they are crucial allies in supporting the youngster. This degree of commitment from the responsible adult is a basic prerequisite. Children drop out of treatment if a pessimistic or demoralized adult discourages them from attending.

Many adults who seek assistance for their children are engaged in some intervention themselves. Services for youngsters following a violent death have been developed by local peer led support groups where the adult has felt helped. They feel sufficiently restored from the violent dying that they now want other family members to join in their restorative retelling. Separate services for youngsters may be offered during the same time that the adults attend group or individual support. Thus, multiple members of the same family are involved in separate but coordinated interventions in the same center. Unfortunately, this innovative approach has not been researched or documented. There is very little published literature on these programs beyond a description of their organization.

Once engaged, children and adolescents are usually in treatment for a longer time than adults. Children require longer-term support and follow up because their distress over the violent dying and their imaginary connection with the deceased continues to resurface as they negotiate subsequent developmental transitions. The memory of the dying and death remains and evokes more distress and poignancy with a more mature realization of the trauma of the violent dying and the finality of the loss. Some children cannot engage in a restorative retelling until they are adults. Maturity and restorative retelling cannot be forced.

Child service agencies have recently extended these individual and group interventions into the schools where teachers and counselors and parents identify vulnerable children who might need support after the violent death of a friend or family member. These school-based programs offer a convenient setting for youngsters, but rarely involve parents or responsible adult family members in a concurrent program of support. Isolating an intervention for youngsters separate from adult family members after a violent dying may be sufficient, but the integrity of the family depends on the stability of a responsible adult. Restoration usually begins by restoring the primary adult caregiver within the family, and extends from there to other family members.

☐ Evidence of Effectiveness

A team of child therapists has published a series of studies documenting their work with youngsters after violent death. Their early studies described school age children who had been exposed to a shooting death within a school (Pynoos, 1987). Later they reviewed and included their clinical experience with young children who had witnessed the homicidal death of a parent (Eth & Pynoos, 1994). They initiated a systematic screening and intervention for all the youngsters to establish which children were at greatest risk for maladaptive responses through a time-limited assessment within the classroom (Eth & Pynoos, 1985). Their studies verified that youngsters who were actual witnesses of the killing, or had not witnessed the killing, but were emotionally attached to the deceased, were particularly vulnerable. They devised a time-limited supportive intervention for children who were highly distressed and measured its favorable outcome (Pynoos & Nader, 1988, 1990).

Presumably, this work served as a basis for the initiation of school based support programs after violent death developed in many major urban communities during the last decade. Unfortunately, it is rare for these newly developed services to maintain the same rigor in assessment and agenda of treatment recommended by its originators.

Their structured assessment and intervention has been applied with other populations of youngsters who have been collectively exposed to violent dying with natural disasters and war, with similar findings of risk and response to short-term intervention. While these findings are highly impressive, they do not include comparative measures from an untreated control group.

As with time-limited group interventions with adults, this systematic intervention is of limited use to the individual clinician or youngster. It requires a specialized clinic staffed by clinicians with sophisticated measures for assessment and extensive experience with techniques of individual, group and family intervention.

☐ Guidance for Parents and Caregivers

Parents or other responsible adults in a family where there has been a violent death are sometimes over-determined to find their children professional help. Their concern is a sure sign of their caring, but may be based on their unresolved fear of the dying and their dread of its long-ranging effects, instead of sure signs of distress in their child. When an adult asks me for guidance I try to understand what his or her child needs, and I have no hesitation in arranging a referral, but I also try to gauge the adult's resilience and potential as a listener for restorative retelling. After all, it is the adult who is a major support figure for the child, and I want to foster a restorative alliance between them.

"How do I know when my child needs help?"

I try to be reassuring to parents in emphasizing that very few children require formal treatment after a violent death of a family member, yet the very fact that they are questioning their child's emotional needs is a good sign. Their concern signals their attunement to what their child is confronting. There are rare circumstances when immediate clinical assessment and reinforcement of resilience and retelling is probably warranted, such as when there have been multiple deaths, or the child has actually witnessed the killing. However, with time and assurance of surrounding stability and support, children usually accommodate to a violent death.

"What your child needs most is a confidence that she is safe and that you are safe too." Parents' concern for their child is an important ingredient for restoration and a sign that they are not likely to minimize or avoid their child's distress.

"What can I do to help my child through this?"

"What your child needs is your patience and willingness to listen to what he or she is telling himself/herself about the dying."

This is an opening for outlining the model of restorative retelling that an adult and child in the family can carry out together. Children may be encouraged to talk openly about the dying by recognizing that everyone in the family has been left with their own story and it is safe and acceptable for them to retell their own story to an adult when they need to. This is not to suggest that the adult should use the child as a listener—the adult should save that for another adult. Listening to the distressing possessions of parents or other caregivers after a violent death does not comfort children. Children are comforted in knowing that thoughts of reenactment and possessive fears and feelings of grief are common to everyone, and that someone responsible for them recognizes their retelling as safe and predictable. This explanation, that retelling is normal and purposeful, may loosen their resistance to retelling within and without the family. It also provides the responsible adult with a direct way to listen for the level of trauma and separation distress within the story that the child retells, without memorizing or referring to lists of maladaptive signs or symptoms. It is far more natural, and potentially restorative, for the adult to periodically inquire and listen to their youngster's retelling. I want the adult to maintain his or her role as patient listener rather than questioning diagnostician.

"When should I get professional help for my child?"

"Wait for a couple of months after the death, because the chances are good that most of your child's distress will clear within that time. If your child's distress continues to interfere with his or her functioning at home or school or in his or her friendships, arrange for an assessment with a clinician who knows something about the effects of violent death."

The decision to proceed with therapy is complex because children do not directly ask for it. Therapy cannot begin or succeed without their cooperation, or the commitment of the responsible adult, and the "good enough" fit of the clinician's assessment and approach. All of these variables are difficult to gauge until everyone meets. The decision may pivot on subjective reactions of *"I'm not ready for this."* or *"I'm not comfortable with this therapist."* more than objective criteria of risk or professional qualifications. Finding the right therapist at the right time may take some time and searching.

"What should I know about the therapist and the therapy?"

The adult needs to have confidence in the qualifications and experience of the clinician. He or she should inquire directly about the therapist's training and experience with violent dying before scheduling an appointment.

I would discourage anyone from seeing a clinician who refuses to meet with the adult responsible for the child. It is important that the adult has a periodic opportunity to meet or communicate with the clinician to monitor the progress of treatment and learn how they might be more supportive.

It is also important at the outset to inquire about the anticipated length of treatment. If the clinician immediately recommends long-term treatment, the responsible adult should understand the clinician's reasons for that recommendation, and then seek a second opinion. Long-term treatment might be appropriate for some particularly vulnerable children, but the adult needs to be assured of its advisability before agreeing to such a major commitment of time and money. Treatment can be approached in a more tentative and circumscribed way—to plan on 15 or 20 sessions and reevaluate the level of distress and indications for continued treatment and clarification of longer-term treatment goals, including medication.

II

CLINICAL INTERVENTION

My meeting with Julie's psychiatrist after her dying would have been less confusing if we had recognized my dilemma. Though we were both psychiatrists, neither or us knew how to answer the riddle of her dying. I was possessed by an incessant questioning that searched for an answer to the "why" of her dying. He tried to help by offering a reasoned monologue that only joined him in my possession. Reasoning was our trap. The meeting would have been more restorative for each of us if he had kept us from dissecting her dying. Instead, he might have shared in my confusion, saying:

"I will try to tell you what I know about her dying, as long as you recognize that I'm left with an unanswerable question myself. None of us can explain her violent dying. Not even Julie could give us an answer that we would accept."

He wouldn't need to say that so directly. He could convey our uncertainty about her dying as we talked about Julie as a person, and not just her dying. She would not be ignored.

We would invoke our memory of Julie when she was alive, and together we could help each other remember her in a restorative way.

I needed this guidance toward an awareness of her living. We should have found that place together rather than my finding it myself in his parking lot.

We were not to blame for our ignorance. As psychiatrists who dealt with the effects of separation and dying on a daily basis in our practices, there was little in our training or professional literature that prepared us for the effects of violent dying. There was no model or scheme to guide us.

Since Julie's death there has been progressively more written on violent dying, and occasional opportunities for training, but most clinicians remain uninformed and unprepared to help someone after a violent death. Out of my own experience of confusion and ignorance, I have tried to develop guidelines that would make intervention more restorative.

In this section of the book I propose a tentative model of coherence and a clinical approach for the clinician and the person who seeks treatment. I emphasize the word *tentative* because it is my goal to instill an attitude of tolerance for uncertainty and ambiguity about violent dying. I use the word *coherence* to instill my goal to reinforce living rather than to promote an objective analysis of dying and death. This model is based upon a changing of perspective: to accept our ultimate uncertainty about violent dying, and divert us toward a living engagement.

Such a model, based upon an active disengagement from searching for certainty, cannot pretend a rigorous objectivity. Though I include the speculations and empirical observations of researchers of violent death (and there is more speculation than data), the model of coherence reaches beyond the objective event and effects of the dying. The goal of coherence is the reestablishment of meaning, and meaning is necessarily subjective and hard to count.

Model of Restorative Retelling

It would be reassuring to cite an extensive list of research studies that document the effectiveness of a specific model of treatment after a violent death. Unfortunately, there have been very few well-designed studies. Under ideal circumstances therapy research is exceedingly difficult to design and complete, and nearly impossible after a violent death. Family members are so traumatized and avoidant, they are hesitant to seek treatment or volunteer for study.

There are a small number of well-designed studies that are not of much relevance for the general reader or practitioner. Those studies, reviewed in the next chapter, measure the effects of a highly specialized treatment (time-limited group therapy). When treated with this intervention, family members show significantly less distress on standardized measures than family members who are not treated. Though this intervention has proven effectiveness, it is offered in a limited number of specialty clinics.

Open-ended support groups or individual psychotherapy are more common treatments after violent dying, but have not been tested. While they may be as effective as time-limited group therapy, and perhaps more effective in providing long-term support, there has been no comparative study.

In the absence of objective data, our understanding of how to treat someone after violent death begins by posing some very basic questions:

What can therapy, any sort of therapy, provide after a violent death?

What can the clinician offer, and the family member anticipate, as essential to effective therapy?

☐ Essentials of Therapy

Therapy is a very vague term that refers to a multitude of approaches and explanatory schemes. Jerome Frank, a distinguished psychiatric researcher, devoted his career to a comprehensive and objective inquiry of psychological therapies. He clarified those elements of psychotherapy essential to success in a short list (Frank & Frank, 1991):

1. A confiding relationship.
2. A healing setting.
3. A rational scheme with a plausible explanation of symptoms.
4. The participation of subject and therapist, in an active procedure, believed by both to be the means of restoring health.

A clinician in every successful therapy instills these factors. Group therapy, individual therapy, family therapy, interpersonal therapy, psychoanalytic therapy, cognitive therapy, behavioral therapy, paradoxical therapy, trauma therapy, grief therapy (there are hundreds more) pivot around an essential confidence and trust in a clinician who provides comfort and safety from distress, who actively explains how and why health has been lost, and who shares in a procedure for restoring it.

While family, friends, and clergy may offer support through a confiding relationship and healing setting, they do not offer a rational explanation for prolonged distress, or a reliable procedure to restore health. They recognize their limitations when their efforts to soothe and heal are ineffective, but rarely recommend treatment when their efforts have failed.

When people ask for therapy after a violent death, they do so in spite of considerable social and personal resistance. After all, death, even violent death, is a natural consequence of living. Something as inevitable as grief and trauma, it is commonly believed, should subside with time. Unfortunately, when the inevitable responses persist or worsen with time, there is no inevitable solution.

By the time family members seek therapy, they may be very troubled. They have been unable to quiet their imaginary reenactment and possession of the dying and need more than a patient listener. They are probably in a state of persistent fear and confusion of violent dying and seek someone who can restore them from what has happened. They want to find a way to quiet themselves.

Since this book emphasizes the processing of violent death as a narrative, it would follow that the first priority for the clinician would be to elicit and listen to the dying story. Not so. Whoever asks for help probably cannot help themselves while retelling. They are so preoccupied with retelling, to the media and police and friends and coworkers, that they haven't found time for themselves and their own living story.

A clinical priority within the first interview is to find out if the dying reenactment continues as a vivid and traumatic intrusion in daily living. If survivors are forced to devote more of themselves to the intrusive dying story than their own living, they need to be protected and diverted from their reenactment possession.

☐ Resilience First

Instead of retelling, the first priority is crisis intervention, another term for reinforcing resilience. A sense of safety and separateness from the reenactment drama needs to be established (Rynearson, 1996).

The clinician first instills resilience by *being* resilient through an active attitude of support and clarification that is calming. It is reassuring for the family member to hear that the clinician is more concerned about their person than their story. If retelling the story is imperative, of course the clinician listens, but interrupts when the story absorbs too much time or becomes too distressing. By interrupting, the clinician creates a dialogue to divert the teller from the ruinous monologue in which the teller plays no role.

Within this resilient focus, the clinician and the family member create a constructive agenda and bearing. There will be a time to deal with the violent dying when the family member is more resilient and stabilized, and in actively delaying retelling, the clinician emphasizes that avoidance may serve a constructive purpose (Raphael & Minkov, 1999). First, the family member's resources and capacity for resilience may be explored through a series of constructive, open-ended questions:

"Is there someone available who will support you, right now?" If so, that person may become a valuable ally in counseling, and the clinician considers including him or her in this early phase of resilience reinforcement—even later in the introductory session if the person is in the waiting area.

"What has helped you in the past after a death or a trauma?" This question is not inviting a detailed trauma history, but an insight into what has fostered this person's resilience. Was it family? Work? A strong spiritual belief? Taking care of someone else? Or a pet? This may lead to a useful inventory of resilient activities, beliefs and contacts.

"What do you need to help you through this?" Some family members have a clear idea of what they need, or they may be concerned about the needs of other family members. There are fundamentals for survival (a safe place to stay, food, transportation, and finances) essential for the entire family. If there is an investigation or trial of the death, victims'

services and advocacy can be requested. This question is an invitation to join the clinician in organizing a list of resilient resources.

"What would (the name of the person who died violently) say that you needed now?" This question has a restorative purpose. It places the clinician and the family member in a reunion fantasy beyond the ruinous death, and tries to enliven the deceased as a helper. The fantasized answer usually carries a strong message of warmth and forgiveness and leads to memories of safety and separateness to counterbalance the image of violent dying.

The answers to this kind of constructive questioning are not more important than the attitude conveyed—that together we can find a way to feel safer and more alive. This is very different than the data-driven questioning imposed by the task of arriving at a diagnosis. The highly distressed family member doesn't need a diagnosis. He or she needs immediate care to be more resilient. Diagnosis can come later.

☐ Strategies to Reinforce Resilience: The 3 P's

Since the sense of safety and separateness are preverbal experiences, it is difficult to convey them with words (Rose, 1987).

I illustrate my private image of resilience as floating on the surface of a strong tide where I can breathe and remain calm and flow with the current until it has spent itself. This image came from a physical experience that showed me how to survive an overwhelming stress. Now I can speculate that its vividness and my fear may have activated all of my memory systems—procedural, episodic, and finally semantic as I write about it. At first, floating and suspending myself on the surface of an undertow was not a verbal or symbolic experience. It registered at a level that was fundamentally physical.

There are three separable resilient capacities within my resilient image:

1. *Pacification* is the most primary and refers to the capacity for self-calming or soothing. It is essential as a basis for limiting the primal experience of disintegrating terror.
2. *Partition* refers to the capacity for self-discrimination. It is essential in establishing a limitation or boundary between the experiential worlds of "me" and "not me."
3. *Perspective* refers to the capacity for self-transcendence. It is essential in allowing time to penetrate experience so change can be anticipated.

These **3 P's** comprise a useful scheme for the functions of resilience. Reconsidering my own resilient image—as I became terrified of drowning

I first had to *pacify* myself from my terror, before I could allow myself to *partition* myself from the depths by floating, and finally gain a *perspective* that I could remain suspended on the surface until a future time when the current would diminish. This progression of the 3 P's can be applied with the family member who is overwhelmed by the story of violent dying—first to pacify their terror, then to partition themselves from merging with the dying imagery, and finally to regain their perspective that time will bring change by their transcending and prevailing.

The factors of effective therapy (a confiding relationship, a healing setting, and an active scheme and procedure for restoration) are roughly analogous to the 3P's of individual resilience. The clinician and family member join in a comforting relationship (pacification) in a safe setting (partition) and engage in a restorative scheme and procedure (perspective).

Early Restoration

Another less direct reinforcement of resilience can be summoned with memories of the deceased before their death. These are memories that contain a storehouse of vital imagery to counterbalance the dying images of reenactment. During the initial session these positive images help in beginning a constructive focus:

"Tell me about (first name of the person who died violently)?" This retelling is encouraged rather than interrupted. The goal is to vivify that person's presence as a constructive basis for a restorative story. Often the positive memories of the deceased have been overwhelmed by reenactment fantasies, and it is restoring to reclaim them.

"Do you have any pictures of (first name of the person who died violently)?" At this point a picture is retrieved from a wallet or purse and the passing and viewing of that living image includes the clinician in a nonverbal, restorative reunion. This may begin to counterbalance the agonized image of the deceased in the reenactment fantasy. After a violent dying that involves mutilation, this summoning of a smiling and "shining" image (the usual image with a posed picture) can be sustaining to the family member.

"How would (first name of the person who died violently) feel about your asking for help?" This is another projective question that tries to summon the image of the deceased as a supportive ally in counseling. The answer is usually affirming.

Format for Resilience and Restoration

By the end of the initial interview the clinician has become more active in educating the family member about resilience and restoration and the priority of reinforcing them. The primary goal of resilience and restoration is clearly stated:

> *"Right now we need to help you adjust to this tragedy by calming and clearing your mind of the dying."* If the family member has been overwhelmed with reenactment fantasies and intense trauma there are several brief and simple assignments:
>
> *"I want you to interrupt your thoughts of their dying with thoughts of their living."*
>
> *"The flashback of the dying is very common, like a story you can't stop telling yourself, and it will subside as we help you retell more of their living and less of their dying."*
>
> *"I want you to repeat the relaxation exercises every day and begin to gather pictures and reminders of (first name of the person who died violently) before our next visit so you can tell me more about them."*

This format provides a reconstructive structuring for the task of early retelling. Since family members are invariably processing the dying as a story, they understand the narrative model and its goal. The narrative model assumes an active role in beginning a more coherent retelling.

When they return for their second session, family members are often laden with photo albums or articles belonging to the deceased, writings or videotapes of the loved one's last birthday—whatever they choose to bring These are the objects or images that connect the clinician with the deceased as they are presented and handled in commemoration. The clinician is privileged to serve as witness and celebrant of their life and "presence" that has now been included in the counseling.

After the commemorative presentation, the clinician and the family member are more engaged because the session has usually been filled with strong feeling for the deceased. There may be a sense of lightness because some of the burden of the dying story has lifted.

Within this growing calmness there is time to ask more directly about attitudes toward death.

The belief in an after-life promises a release from dying and a reunion with the deceased as a story in the future that is comforting to foretell. It points towards a constructive experience. Those who deny such a belief rarely feel handicapped by its absence, and usually disregard its relevance. Others are more tentative and curious about death and are not satisfied with the ultimacy of a belief or a denial.

Regardless of their attitude, it is common for the family member who is closely identified with the violent death to now question their own mortality. For the clinician, knowing and respecting the family member's concept of death offers a deeper understanding of the dynamics of the death experience.

Crisis Resolution

This early reinforcement of resilience and restorative retelling may begin a progressive return of self-confidence and autonomy that brings relief. Reenactment fantasies are less frequent and absorbing and trauma distress is reduced. Several follow-up sessions may further consolidate these changes towards a restorative retelling.

At this point, the family member and clinician may consider a provisional "break" from counseling. The clinician emphasizes their availability for future appointments, if reenactment imagery and trauma distress should recur. They are advised that separation distress might increase now that the trauma distress has reduced, but that is a more familiar distress for them to manage.

☐ Treatment Evaluation

Community studies have documented that crisis counseling after trauma is relatively brief—an average of only 10 or 15 sessions (New & Berliner, 2000). If someone requires more assistance, he or she is probably presenting with a combination of risk factors, and needs to be assessed for a more comprehensive treatment (Rynearson & Geoffrey, 1999).

Demographic Risk Factors

These are unalterable variables that can be reliably and directly documented—and several are associated with prolonged distress and treatment seeking (Rynearson, 1995):

Age: By itself, age is not an accurate predictor for treatment, but its interaction with kinship (young mothers or old widowers) is highly predictive of persistent distress and disorder.

Gender: Women score higher on self-report measures of distress, and out-number men by a 4:1 ratio in seeking treatment after a violent death.

Kinship: Mothers, followed by fathers, are most distressed and most commonly seek treatment after the violent death of a child.

Mode of Death: Homicide, suicide and accidental dying, while highly stressful, are associated with a descending order of intensity on self-report measures of distress.

Income: Income is negatively correlated with distress—the less income, the more distress.

These demographic variables suggest a composite that would be highly predictive of treatment seeking—a young, financially and emotionally distressed mother, after the homicidal death of her child.

Personal Risk Factors

These are variables that are associated with inherent or acquired vulnerabilities that may worsen distress and disorder, and increase the need for treatment.

Comorbidity: The presence of a psychiatric disorder (most frequently Anxiety, Major Depression, or Substance Abuse Disorder) is associated with prolonged dysfunction and treatment seeking.

History of Psychological Treatment: Previous treatment (outpatient or inpatient) is associated with higher distress and treatment seeking.

Childhood Abuse and Neglect: The history of childhood abuse and neglect during crucial phases of neuro-psychological development often results in impaired resilience and dysfunctional responses to trauma and separation.

Degree of Attachment: Intense attachment with the person who died violently is correlated with increased trauma and separation distress and treatment seeking.

With the addition of these variables, a composite of even greater vulnerability would now include—a young, financially and emotionally distressed mother, with a developmental history of abuse and neglect, who has been intermittently treated for Depression and PTSD and Substance Abuse, who was overly-dependent on her 17 year old son who was murdered.

This composite would signal that this young woman carried a powerful combination of serious problems long before her son's murder. Each of those antecedent distresses and disorders was probably stirred by the murder and their combination presents as a snarl rather than a series of problems.

Family Assessment

Since the entire family shares in accommodating the violent death of a family member, it is important for the clinician to gauge their shared capacity for resilience and retelling. Involving the family at the beginning of treatment, to encourage their support and clarify their questions, is so natural that it is insensitive to do otherwise. Family members usually want to be included, or at least to be invited.

I prepare the individual and the family for assessment by emphasizing that we are not gathering for family therapy. This is not the time or place to stir unresolved conflicts or frustrations. Our goal is to help the family as an interactive unit in hearing and respecting the uniqueness of each restorative retelling. During the family assessment, I outline strategies for diminishing distress and the simple model of restorative retelling for everyone to hear. I suggest that they actively listen to one another as they retell their own version of the violent dying while sitting together in my office. The family is often startled at the differences, and sometimes disparity, in what they have imagined. This can serve as a working illustration of their mutuality in retelling and revising the dying story as a family.

Often the family member who asks for treatment retells his or her story of the death with more intense distress and remorse or reenactment than the others. The other family members can re-orient their retelling to include memories of the living relationship with the deceased. The family offers a rich repository of memories of the deceased when he or she was alive and hopeful, an important resource for the clinician to tap and for the family to share.

At the end of the session, I thank everyone for their help and reserve the option to call them in again. If other family members request treatment, I refer them to another clinician. I explain that since each retelling is unique, I save my attention and retelling for one family member at a time. I might become confounded, and even dubious, listening to simultaneous but separate retellings of the same event.

There are at least two circumstances when I recommend family therapy at the outset. One is when the family is so avoidant and frightened of the dying that they cannot begin retelling during the assessment. I invite them to return so I can at least catalyze their starting and this can usually be accomplished with several sessions. The second is when the family has been forced to adjust to an intra-family death (where one family member has caused the death of another). They are so torn by their shared identification with both the deceased and the perpetrator, that their capacities for resilience and retelling are overwhelmed. Intra-family violent dying is profoundly stressful and it is difficult for the family to maintain a sense of trust and safety during its retelling. These families are at high risk for disintegrating—particularly after a homicide—and may have been highly dysfunctional before the death. In my experience, such a family avoids treatment despite their intense need for support and restoration.

Psychological Testing

There are many brief, standardized, reliable, self-report measures that document the presence and severity of anxiety, depression or substance abuse. Testing for these disorders can be pivotal to management. If they verify the presence of a disorder of depression, anxiety, or substance abuse, then additional consultation for medication or more specialized treatment for anxiety or substance abuse is initiated. Several brief, self-report measures may screen for these disorders and details for obtaining them are included in the Appendix.

At present, there is no validated test to verify the presence or severity of combined trauma and separation distress after a violent death. There is a self-report measure that has been recently developed for traumatic grief (the Inventory of Traumatic Grief, Prigerson, 1995) but this measure has not been applied to subjects after violent dying.

An objective measure of resilience would also be clinically useful, but is not yet available.

Psychiatric Consultation

When a family member carries a combination of demographic and personal risk factors (particularly the high probability of a coexistent psychiatric disorder) a consultation with a psychiatrist can begin a more comprehensive treatment. The pharmacological treatment of a severe anxiety or depressive disorder is an important ancillary to treatment (Shuchter & Zisook, 1996). Several well-designed studies show that bereaved subjects with psychiatric disorders have a better outcome when their psychotherapy is combined with the judicious use of medication (Jacobs, 1999). Medication does not directly influence grief, which is treated with continued psychotherapy or counseling; however, medication has a significant clinical effect on the underlying disorder. Indeed, there is evidence that individuals with severe depression or anxiety who remain untreated with medication are at high risk for remaining disabled (Zisook & Shuchter, 1996).

Suicide is an infrequent complication, but when it occurs and the clinician failed to consider consultation for pharmacotherapy, they are vulnerable to a charge of clinical negligence. However, after a violent death, family members who require medication for a comorbid psychiatric disorder need concurrent therapy for their traumatic grief; a medical doctor or psychiatrist who treats a family member with nothing but medication would be negligent as well.

Past History of Treatment

It is not enough to record the diagnosis and dates and types of therapy. Knowing that a family member took psychotropic medication, saw an individual therapist for six months, or attended group therapy for domestic violence, or chemical dependency treatment for over a year, is significant but does not provide much insight. A more dynamic understanding of his or her therapy experience, again, comes from open-ended questioning. Following are some valuable open-ended questions.

Why did you start therapy—what did you need to change?

Was therapy a way for them to change something they viewed as external or internal? As an example, therapy for domestic violence may begin by initiating external changes (safe housing, police protection, divorce proceedings) but hopefully included internal changes as well (heightened self-respect, self-efficacy and recognition that abuse was probably tolerated in their primary family). Without some insightful, internal change, they are at risk for beginning another abusive relationship.

What have you learned about yourself from your therapy?

The way of arriving at an answer can be more revealing than the answer itself—from the shallow "I need to control my anger," to the oblivious "nothing," to the discriminating, "that's hard to answer—where do you want me to start?" Each way of answering will give insight into the impact of therapy and the person's involvement and initiative. These are important to assess, because without involvement and initiative there can be little therapeutic movement or change.

Have you considered returning to your previous therapist?

This may be a suggestion as well as a question. If the person had a productive course of treatment and terminated with the therapist, rather than "dropping out," why hasn't he or she considered returning? The clinician is wise to obtain permission to talk with the previous therapist to assist in the transition of treatment and to learn if there were treatment resistances that might be anticipated.

Treatment Limitations and Goals

What changes do we want to work toward with your treatment?

Can the family member summarize what he or she needs, beyond accommodating himself or herself to the violent death? This is not only an opportunity for the family member to clarify his or her therapy goals, but for the clinician to clarify the limits of therapy. If the family member and clinician mutually agree that treatment goals include consultation for a comorbid psychiatric disorder, or long-term problems of childhood abuse or neglect, or substance abuse, or destructive relationships, or an underlying character problem (and the list can be much longer), now is the time when the clinician either agrees to assume the role of solo therapist or recommends a more focused treatment. Most family members and clinicians are unwilling to commit themselves to the long-term, intensive therapy that complex cases often require. Instead, complex cases require combined treatments, and a preliminary treatment plan is a list of problems and specialized resources—medication, supportive therapy for childhood abuse, substance abuse treatment, marital therapy, etc.

It is more sensible to manage a complex treatment with assistance. Acknowledging at the outset that *"we are going to need help from others"* keeps a clinician from assuming the unrealistic role of primary caregiver.

☐ Therapy Goals

The list of therapy goals after a violent death is short and its focus is more circumscribed. There are three primary goals (Bonanno & Kaltman, 1999) and these are extensions and elaborations of the 3 P's that served as a foundation in previous sessions for crisis intervention.

Moderation of Distress and Disorder

This has a more inclusive purpose than pacification because it includes, but extends beyond, the simple encouragement of self-comforting. Treatment offers a rational scheme and a plausible explanation for a beginning insight. The clinician actively explains the difference between trauma and separation distress—and how distress differs from disorder (Rynearson, 1994). Distress and disorder are linked to previous experiences of trauma and separation to form an insightful understanding of why these experiences have been so overwhelming. They may have been unsupported and isolated with their previous experience of trauma and separation, and the clinician now serves as the patient, reassuring and clarifying ally that they so sorely needed. However, the purpose of this inquiry is to gain a mastery of the recent event of violent death and not to become absorbed by the unfulfilled needs of the past. The clinician actively guides this inquiry to develop more adaptive responses that moderate the threat of violent death. There are several clinical techniques and strategies through which mastery can begin:

Pacification — Self-comforting is restored and reinforced through physical actions that encourage *relaxation*. Progressive loosening of various muscles groups, accompanied by deep breathing and meditation, are timeless techniques. Self-comforting may also include guided imagery exercises that suggest a tranquil setting. Moderation of distress and the realization of survival begin within this awareness of inner calmness.

Partition — Autonomy from the dying is reclaimed through imaginary exercises and tangible behaviors that reestablish self-security and territoriality. The awareness of a private domain or space—a "where" for the self—is fundamental for autonomy. A search for an inner space that can be buttressed with comforting images and memories is actively pursued by *cognitive* exercises that substitute negative or traumatic thoughts with thoughts that bring self-confidence and independence. *Behavioral* exercises that encourage self-assured conduct provide a tangible experience of self-effectiveness to replace inactions of submission and helplessness.

Perspective — Self-transcendence is the capacity of the stabilized and autonomous self to reorient itself to a space and time beyond the unbearable immediacy of the trauma. In this reorientation, the self maintains a connection to, but distance from, the trauma, where it can observe and become an agent for change. This gives a vantage point for constructive self-reintegration, where there is time for a dynamic mastery of the trauma. Perspective is reflected in the attitude and role of the clinician who can share the space and time of distress—but who remains calm and observant and confident that the family member can share a space and time of perspective as well. Perspective is more directly reinforced by the procedure of *re-exposure*, by which the clinician and family member are able to reenact and retell the dying drama together. The dying drama can be retold through the more concrete exercises of art, writing, or in the actual visitation and viewing of the death scene together. Now the dying drama can be retold from a more detached and calmer vantage point with the stabilizing presence of the clinician and the enlivened memory of the deceased.

Perspective is the most encompassing and inclusive of the resilient capacities and is essential in actively narrating a dying story that can be widened, deepened and interconnected with other memories.

Techniques of *psychotherapy* (analytic, insight oriented, interpersonal, existential, self therapy, etc.) consider self-transcendence to be a fundamental goal of treatment, but these psychotherapies are not specifically designed for the treatment of trauma or impaired resilience.

Therapies designed for intervention after overwhelming trauma (e.g., for combat veterans, rape victims, victims of physical and sexual abuse) include techniques for relaxation and cognitive-behavioral modification because they are effective in reinforcing preverbal resilience. These therapies are focused, brief and are effective after overwhelming trauma (Foa & Meadows, 1997), but they have not been systematically studied in subjects traumatized by a violent death. Since they have a proven effectiveness with severe trauma distress they would presumably offer comparable relief with traumatized family members.

Several trauma-based therapies make highly speculative claims of neurobiologic specificity through Eye Movement Desensitization and Reprocessing (EMDR; Solomon & Shapiro, 1997), and Thought Field Therapy (TFT; Callahan & Callahan, 1997). These therapies are based upon the inclusive use of familiar techniques of relaxation and cognitive-behavioral modification. Additional techniques of saccadic eye movements, or cutaneous pressure points, are presumed to enhance the neuro-biologic integration of traumatic memories. It is not surprising that improvement would follow treatments that are so thorough in applying proven techniques. Recent studies have shown that rapid eye movements are not necessary or related to improvement while following the EMDR protocol (Pitman, Orr, & Altman, 1996). The effectiveness of EMDR or TFT is most probably related to their intense, multisensory format that activates multiple affects and cognitions, with a high degree of anticipation that improvement will follow.

There are too many claims of "curing where others have failed" from too many therapies to take any one claim seriously. Most have some degree of success, but it is difficult to validate which is most effective. The reader is wise to maintain a healthy skepticism about such claims, and the clinician should have a solid working knowledge of several techniques rather than a dogmatic insistence on a single approach.

Continuing the Relationship with the Deceased

The violent death of a loved one differs from other traumas because it presents additional distress to the loss. The physical presence of the deceased is irreversibly gone. There is no further opportunity to connect— to reach for or be reached by the family member. The dynamic touching of shared living stops.

Of course the relationship stops, and it doesn't. Family members continue to reach for and be touched by the persistent memory of whoever died. The relationship continues as a deep and wide remembrance of shared experiences. Memories of physical (procedural) and preverbal (episodic) experience in the relationship are as intense as verbal (semantic) memories—particularly in parents who shared nurturing experiences that were purely physical and preverbal during infancy and early childhood. That is why the memory can return with a familiar glance, gesture, touch, odor, song, or taste. Each of these physical cues can be intimately connected with the living memory before death. At first these preverbal memories are intensely recalled and summon the more figurative memory of the deceased.

This is a conscious reflection of a powerful neurobiologic response. The awareness that a family member is "lost" is disruptive to the smooth and balanced processing of thoughts, feelings, and behaviors. Involuntary scanning and searching for the lost person is screened by memory systems that sharpen and augment awareness for any clue that would help in finding them. Unlike the avoidance of violent dying, separation draws family members towards a restoring of their living connection. Longing and searching are involuntary actions to reestablish a comforting and stabilizing attachment.

Approaching and reconstructing an attachment with the vibrant memory of the deceased becomes less intense with time. There is probably enough self-comforting and stabilization within the fantasized re-attachment to diminish the longing and searching. The memory of the person remains, but recedes, and family members continue to remember. Eventually, remembrance becomes more implicit and is provoked by specific reminders of that person (his or her birthday, picture, or hand writing), then fades from awareness until another reminder summons it. The potential experience of relatedness returns with each remembrance. The memory is not extinguished nor the relationship forgotten. That person's memory continues as a private attachment bringing continual comfort and stability. Whether it is implicit or recalled, it is always there.

More rarely, the memory of the deceased remains intensely explicit and carries a fixed, internalized relatedness—or possession. When possessed, the family member cannot release himself or herself from an attempt to reattach—a dictate of reuniting with their living or undoing their violent dying. The possessive fantasies and behaviors of reuniting and undoing are usually exaggerations of the family member's characteristic role with the deceased.

Unlike reenactment possession (where there is no role for the family member), in the narratives of possession they are primary players in the dying and death. There are at least four separable relational possessions to consider, but they may occur in combination:

1. *Possession of Reuniting.* Those possessed with reuniting have an overdetermined need to remember and relate to the deceased. They are preoccupied with finding and reestablishing their attachment. A disproportionate degree of thought, feeling, and behavior is invested in returning to a highly idealized relationship as they imagine existed before the death. This possession has been long recognized by clinicians and grief researchers as *chronic grief*—an inconsolable longing and searching for an idealized relationship, lasting for years rather than months. This response is presumed to be secondary to a disorder of attachment in which the family member was overly dependent upon the relationship for his or her own security.

   It is difficult to intervene in this possessive relatedness without threatening the underlying attachment. Such family members, intent upon reuniting, see their solution in a magical return to, rather than revision of, their relatedness with person who died. These family members are usually quite resistant to viewing their distress as internally derived—if only they could reunite, there would be no distress—and feel threatened at the prospect of a new relationship. Withdrawing from their persistent attachment would leave them feeling abandoned and vulnerable. Others in the family sometimes feel burdened by the attachment demands that are now displaced to them, and they often insist on counseling.

2. *Possession of Remorse.* Those possessed with remorse relate to the broken attachment as if it were a personal failure. Instead of engaging with and feeling comforted by the memory of the deceased, they obsess about their own carelessness in preventing the violent death. They are often left with a tyranny of shoulds (I should have . . . , or I should not have. . . .) that ends in the same bramble of self-condemnatory thought, feeling, and behavior. Their need to undo the dying and death by continuing in such a highly controlling role keeps them from a comforting remembrance. When they remember the deceased they feel inordinate guilt about their personal irresponsibility and shame in the exposure of their failure. This possession is exhausting because its

focus and energy is self-abusive, and it is difficult to feel deserving of help or assistance.

As with reunion, there is a fantasized undoing of the dying, but in remorseful possession there is an active effort to revise the self, though that revision is destructive. Dying and death are not denied, and the self is not magically preserved in a remorseful relatedness. The family member accepts the reality of the violent dying and death but attempts to sacrifice himself or herself as atonement for what has happened. The ultimate atonement for remorse is the fantasized substitution of oneself for the deceased. It is common for the remorseful family member to repeatedly say, "I'm the one who should have died."

There is the possibility of a more constructive self-revision in this possession, because there is a role for the self in the narrative. The family member assumes a role for himself or herself that is connected with the person's living memory as well as his or her dying and death. This offers the clinician a narrative focus that includes the family member in a role that can be modified.

The goal with intervention is to widen the possessed mourner's role in the narrative, to play a more generative and reconstructive part, while decreasing his or her absorption in the sense of failure and shame. This work of self-expansion begins by retelling past experiences when the family member was successful as protector and caregiver. Recalling and elaborating these nurturing memories may be rejuvenating—particularly with parents who remember their years of positive self-sacrifice. Remembering self-sacrifice is accompanied by a spectrum of feelings, including frustration and anger—that the efforts to protect and nurture were disregarded, or unappreciated, and, finally, futile.

Remorse, guilt, and shame have presumably been characteristic responses with these family members long before the violent death. There may have been a history of excessive self-control and immediate self-blame when something stressful occurred. It is relieving for the controlling, remorseful family member to admit that his or her anger and blame may be justified and not entirely self-directed.

3. *Possession of Overprotection*. Those possessed by overprotection relate to the broken attachment as if it were immanent to themselves and surviving family members. They are intensely and persistently apprehensive that violent death is going to recur. Their thoughts, feelings, and behaviors maintain a steady state of high alert and warning to prevent this from happening again. The relatedness is not so much to the memory of the deceased as to the safety of remaining family members who must be protected from the possibility of recurrent dying and death.

In this protective narrative, the family member assumes the role of devoted, but mindless, guard. His or her protectiveness is not connected with the memory of the deceased or the needs of the living who often protest against the intrusive and hovering checking and demands for proximity. The compulsive protectiveness appears to represent a displacement and then reversal of their fear and helplessness: *"I can protect us from what I can't tolerate or prevent (one of us is going to die too)."* Overprotectiveness is a character trait that probably preceded the violent death, and may be associated with a pre-existent compulsive or anxiety disorder.

Such individuals are so involved in an externalized compulsion of prevention that they are not aware of their own distress. Their protective thoughts, feelings, and behaviors are difficult to interrupt because that would risk losing another family member. So long as they are tangibly safe there is less distress. This protective possession is frequent in parents after the violent death of a child. Surviving children are on a very short leash. If they are older, they begin to protest the loss of their own independence and territory.

Family intervention is more effective with protective possession where the entire family can help in devising a protocol of safety together.

4. *Possession of Retaliation.* When those possessed by the urge to retaliate remember the deceased, they feel a cold rage. This rage is directed outward in an intense search for the perpetrator and revenge for the killing. Their thoughts, feelings and behaviors of relatedness with the dying are joined with the investigation and retribution of the police and courts, but they are impatient with the inertia of the system. There is generally a degree of grandiosity in their demands, as if they need to oversee every detail to maintain control.

Their need for revenge and retribution absorbs so much of their attention that it may interfere with their acknowledgement of the death and their own sorrow. They are swept along in a strident demand for action and do not allow themselves to accept their own vulnerability and pain. Perhaps they are trying to restore themselves and their controlling role in the attachment by undoing the helplessness and dishonor of the deceased as they were dying.

Suicidal dying interferes with retaliation. After suicide, retaliatory family members are left enraged by a dying that has no living perpetrator to search out and punish. Of course, there is anger whenever someone commits suicide, but there is no external reinforcement or inquiry against which to retaliate. There are family members who are so enraged and retaliatory that they are unwilling to accept a dying as suicidal. Even when the authorities and other family members disagree, they insist that the dying was homicidal or accidental, and someone must be found and punished.

It is very difficult for the clinician to intervene. Those possessed with retaliation sees themselves as an agent for action—to right what is wrong. In this somewhat omnipotent relatedness, they have little inclination to examine their own role in the dying and death, and any attempt to retell the narrative leads to a recitation of the facts of the investigation or pending trial. They are further enraged with the process of plea-bargaining, or early release if someone is tried and imprisoned, and may begin a bitter retaliation against the criminal-judicial system that failed them. Over-relatedness with revenge and retribution overshadows the memory of the deceased.

The clinician avoids being swept in the narrative of retaliation and indirectly encourages the family member to vent his or her unexpressed sorrow and helplessness. This work can be very tedious. It is difficult to divert someone from his or her role of powerful and controlling retaliator and help them admit to feeling sad and overwhelmed.

Avoidance of Relationship with the Deceased

The most vexing response for the clinician is the family member who shows no distress and claims no relatedness with his or her memory of the violent death.

Avoidance refers to a mental state in which there is a minimal acceptance of the violent death. This is different than denial, where there is a total negation of the experience—as if the violent death never happened. Denial is exceedingly rare in adult family members, although very young children can erase their memory of the violent death and continue an imaginary attachment.

With avoidance, family members are aware of the violent death, but they are in a state of disavowal—they relate to the dying and the death as if it had no effect. Their pattern of thoughts, feelings, and behaviors are unchanged, and their view of themselves and their own future is unaltered. They dismiss any suggestion that the violent death has had a meaningful impact.

It is common for family members to protect themselves with denial and avoidance in the first days and weeks following the violent death. Perhaps this state of total or partial "amnesia" serves as a protective psychological anesthesia to deaden or numb the memory of the violent dying, though family members may be unaware that they have anesthetized themselves. Drugs and alcohol have a similar effect. It is only when denial or avoidance (and sometimes substance abuse) persists for months or years that other family members or friends become concerned over their lack of reactivity or apparent indifference to what has happened. Often, that family member has been avoidant for so many years that its persistence is unnoticed.

Denial and avoidance are both negating and imperceptible. Much is written, but little is truly known, of these negating states. It is difficult to explain or measure this process that diminishes distress and disappears in its own trail. There is a strong and widespread opinion that denial and avoidance are unhealthy and need to be directly challenged, and in some instances that helps. However, a direct challenge is usually ineffective and it is probably unwise to insist on an immediate change until the clinician and the avoidant family member understand its purpose and can replace its function.

There have been no long-term studies of highly avoidant family members after violent death to clarify their outcome. Case reports describe family members whose distress and relatedness with the memory of violent death has surfaced years later (often triggered by a subsequent death experience), but these cases probably represent a minority of family members who remain avoidant and nondistressed.

Despite the many protocols of therapy for intense grief and traumatic intrusion, there are none for the treatment of avoidance as an isolated clinical problem. When avoidance and intrusion present together, as they often do, avoidance diminishes after the active participation of the family member in a procedure of stress reduction and reexposure to reduce intrusion. Avoidance by itself, however, probably has a specific neurobiology and remains resistant to intervention until it spontaneously subsides.

Meaning

The description and definition of meaning can be extremely vague and confusing. Since our purpose is pragmatic and clinical, our focus is limited to a consideration of reestablishing meaning for the family member after a violent death.

An objective inquiry of truth of verifiable facts and logical explanation is not the sort of meaning that is complete, though it is important to the media, the police, and the court. Meaning for the family member includes the subjective rapture of being alive, despite violent death. Subjective meaning allows the family member to balance and join their experience of violent death within their own continuing vitality—to continue living around and through the memory of the dying. Meaning is an extension of perspective, from over absorption in the dying experience, to a solid reconnection with life affirming experience

The subjective meaning of living is dependent on essential values that ensure life—respect, compassion, trust, engagement, altruism. Life-affirming values such as these are merely empty words if not enlivened by action. Violent dying is amoral; it not only lacks but also extinguishes the presence of values through actions of denigration, transgression, destructiveness, and hatred or negligence of life. Violent dying undermines the meaning of living because essential values are disintegrated by the act (Rynearson, 1981). It is difficult to embrace living while identified with an act that is so catastrophic and cruel.

An extreme example of the perplexity of forming a meaningful connection between inconsequential dying and consequential living has been recorded in the oral testimonies of Holocaust survivors. Lawrence Langer (1991) reviewed thousands of audio-visual recordings, and contrasts these oral narratives from the written narratives of survivors. Oral testimonies allow an overwhelming immediacy of the Holocaust memory—untransformed by the style, imagery, chronology, or coherent, moral vision of writing. He suggests that these oral testimonies are a telling of deprival rather than survival, devoid of life-affirming value, and he argues that it is necessary to hear them for what they are; those this identified with their memory of such massive atrocity cannot trust or commit to living again. They have been so dehumanized by the atrocity that they cannot be restored. No matter how they try, they cannot fully reconnect with the rapture of being alive.

However, the drive to find a subjective meaning beyond the dying memory persists. Subjective meaning gives a structure and direction to ongoing living. The structure and direction pivot on two unique human capacities—a conscious ordering of experience through the coherence of language, and a conscious choice in directing action. Consciousness creates a transcendent meaning through symbolic language and elective acts. These life-affirming words and enactments are the foundation of a meaningful restorative narrative. Meaning does not create an ending to the narrative of violent death, but begins a continuing life narrative that includes it.

Language

Violent dying is overwhelming because of its immediacy and physicality. The imaginary reenactment is consuming because the family member has no distance or referent to protect them from the nameless terror.

When terror and violent dying are nameless, they are disintegrating. There is an intimate link between naming, subjective meaning, and restoration (Lakoff & Johnson, 1980). Through naming the terror and retelling the violent dying, a symbol (word) and narrative (coherence) is created that contains the experience independent of its immediacy and physicality. Naming and retelling gives a mediated relation to the experience. In being named and retold, the experience is rendered both present and absent. It is through language that the dying experience becomes suspended and objectified in a matrix of time and space. The experience can be transformed with subjective meaning, through a symbolic and imaginary revision and restoration.

The clinician encourages naming and retelling of the violent death by listening and helping the family member tolerate and contain his or her terror. However, repeatedly naming and retelling the violent death is a form of possession. A restorative retelling includes naming and retelling vital and life-affirming experiences that encompass and counterbalance the dying.

Action

Vitality is expressed and reflected in living interactions. The enactment of nurturance, altruism, and cooperation—buttressed by attitudes of respect and trust—may be active sources of subjective meaning.

As an extreme example, after a violent death, the parent is not only responding to the loss of the child, but to his or her loss of being a caring parent. For some, being a parent may be their major connection with living. They need to care for someone to bring an integrity and coherence to their future, and without that interaction they feel deadened and useless. In this extreme circumstance, the subjective meaning of their living is lost in their overdetermined interaction.

An action directed at violent dying cannot directly include life-affirming values. The parent who is intent on retaliating or protecting is absorbed in reversing or preventing the dying, but in either case, the action is not directed toward living. The clinician can illustrate his or her own sense of futility and impotence in joining these actions that dismiss living, and insist that a sense of commitment to values and to living outside the dying be included in the work of therapy.

To give a more common example, interacting with others in a respectful, honest, and engaging way is a tangible expression of how we ought to be by valuing the life of others. Values are determined more by conscious choice than biologic inheritance. Because they are voluntary, their enactment ensures their reality. It is after we have interacted with someone over time that we can be sure of his or her values—that he or she "walks the walk" instead of just "talks the talk." Words are empty without their demonstration within a relationship.

Beyond the goals of the private retelling of the person's dying and living, restoration reaches outward and away from the narrative memory. Clinicians encourage family members to reengage themselves in generative interactions to restore their meaningful connection with life—outside themselves and their memory of the violent death. The resource for this value-affirming reengagement is always unique—Valerie, Charles, and Barbara found meaning in helping members of their community, while Robert, Ralph, and Pat devoted themselves to nurturing their own reconstituted families, and Maggie no longer clung to her family, but returned to her church and its vital ritual.

After Julie's dying, I also found my own value-affirming relatedness. Fortunately, I have a supportive family that provided most of that affirmation for me. Beyond that, my role of clinician gave a sense of purpose and coherence to my memory of Julie and her dying.

Writing this book and teaching about violent dying is another way to give words and action to counter my own incoherence. Caring for patients, and clarifying the incoherence of violent dying for other clinicians, reestablishes a meaning for my memory of Julie and her dying. That is a way she would want to be remembered.

Specialized Interventions for Restorative Retelling

Years ago, after the violent death of a loved one, highly distressed families helped themselves. Clinicians had no specific interventions, and many family members were frustrated by therapists' inappropriate suggestion—that the family member's anguish was related to some deep-seated problem that had existed long before the violent dying. Families needed more relevant and immediate help, so they began to meet for mutual support.

In the '60s and the '70s, there was a widespread social movement that promoted support groups. Groups of distressed individuals drew together for mutual support around a shared problem—and groups comprised of crime victims, including members distressed by homicide, suicide, and motor vehicular deaths, sprouted within every major urban center. The shared purpose of these groups was political as well as supportive. It may have been the social unrest of the Vietnam era that promoted this element of political activism. When people joined a support group they not only found an audience for their retelling and an opportunity to help others, but an encouragement to enact social changes. By the late '70s, several of these support groups (e.g., Mother's Against Drunk Driving, Parents of Murdered Children, Survivors of Suicide) developed into nationally organized networks of support and activism to help numerous family members and lobby for legislative changes.

The support service in these groups continues to be primarily one of advocacy—advocating for the confused and helpless family member as they confront the media, the police, the victims' assistance regulations, the courts, and sometimes the prisons. Advocacy and activism focus on pragmatic external changes rather than the internal perspective within the memory of the deceased and their dying.

In the 1980s, national legislation provided funding for victims of crime and mandated that police and prosecutorial offices include victims' advocacy services. Major criminal judicial programs throughout our country now offer advocacy for family members during the investigation and trial of a crime, but not beyond. Nor do they provide services for family members after a violent death if the deceased was the perpetrator. The victim's assistance workers have a temporary obligation to support family members during the investigation and trial so they remain cooperative as witnesses and resources for the legal process—not because of a primary concern for their distress.

Peer-led support programs are more comprehensive in their services and offer open-ended, mutual support groups that meet monthly. Members are encouraged to retell what they have experienced from the month before, but there is insufficient time to consider how the violent dying has changed them. The meetings provide support, not treatment, and while highly distressed family members may be empowered through advocacy and activism, that may not be enough to resolve their intense trauma and grief.

☐ Group Interventions for Restorative Retelling: The Criminal Death Support Group and the Restorative Retelling Group

In 1978, I contacted the president of a newly formed support group for family members after violent death in Seattle. I had treated one of their members, and was impressed by the group's commitment to helping one another. After listening, I recognized that we might learn something from one another, so I volunteered to serve as a consultant for their mutual support group. I consulted with several members referred for psychiatric assessment and attended their monthly support group meeting for two years.

As a psychiatrist, I was convinced of the powerful effects of group interaction on therapy, so I joined with enthusiasm and a willingness to learn how these groups helped. I knew that groups offer several unique experiences for the members, and I found them in abundance:

1. **Universality** — every member had lost someone to a violent dying, which instilled camaraderie and diminished stigma.

2. **Altruism** — every member could help every other member, offering an active reciprocity in being helped and helping.
3. **Vicarious learning** — every member's understanding could be enhanced by retelling his or her own story and in listening to the stories of other members.
4. **Cohesiveness** — every member recognized that his or her well-being mattered to the other members, and resultant group morale ensured that "we will all survive this together."

At almost every meeting someone would give a spontaneous testimonial to the group—that this group helped them feel connected and understood. I also noted that it was the same 15 or 20 members who faithfully attended. The consistent group was comprised of the officers of the organization (the meeting was held in the home of the president) and members who had attended the support meetings for several years.

There were transient members who attended 3 or 4 sessions and never returned, and a larger group of individuals who attended only once. Obviously, this type of support group was not for everyone—and it never is. The drop-out rate for support groups or group therapy is high because of the anticipatory anxiety stirred by the prospect of revealing one's private life before a group of strangers. New members need considerable preparation before joining a support group to help them through this transition.

I wondered why some members couldn't leave, and why even more potential members wouldn't join. It seemed that some of the long-term members were absorbed in adjusting to problems unrelated to the violent dying—life long problems of being victimized and isolated from a supportive network—and the support group was serving as a family substitute. Other long-term members who were enraged about the murder and were determined to find retribution and justice for themselves formed a sub group engaged in political and legislative change. The family members who attended for several sessions were able to briefly retell the story of the homicide and left, feeling grateful and relieved.

I was most concerned about the family members who attended for a single meeting and never returned. They were uncomfortable in retelling and listening to other stories of homicide that began every group, for that was the way that each member introduced herself or himself. Some new members were so overwhelmed by listening to the stories of the other members that they bolted from the group to avoid telling their own.

I suspected that a new member who was highly traumatized by the violent death of their own family member could not bear to identify with the trauma contained in the other stories, and didn't feel supported by some member's strident demands for retribution or whining demands for attention. When I shared this impression with the leader of the group, she agreed, and we tried to be more selective in offering the group to those who were less distressed, recommending individual support for the highly traumatized family member before considering support group.

Over the years, my contact with that support group continues, but from a distance. Their leadership has changed (as is the case with most peer-led organizations) so it is difficult to predict what now occurs in their support meetings. There is always an uncertainty about what really happens with peer-led support group interventions because there is no systematic screening for inclusion, no preparation beyond an invitation, and no replicable rationale or agenda or goals with their interaction. An open-ended support group may be open to and welcoming of everyone and willing to consider whatever topics spontaneously surface for as long as the group maintains its focus. With so little structure and even less preparation before joining, finding a support group that fits the needs of every new member is bewildering.

That experience taught me that the group format was a powerful setting for telling and retelling the story of a violent death and provided a rich resource of empathy and resilience. However, I thought its effectiveness could to be enhanced with a more clearly stated focus and purpose. My training in medicine and psychiatry prepared me for following a strategy or protocol in treating a clinical problem. I organized an intervention with a rational agenda and a time-limited format that not only provided the potential group member with a coherent agenda for retelling, but a replicable intervention that could be followed by other clinicians. I was also aware of a natural division in the services of the peer-led support group between advocacy during the investigation and trial and the psychological support for the member's trauma and separation distress that extended above and beyond the crime itself. As a clinician, I was not prepared to assume the role of social activist. Demanding external changes in legislation or the criminal-judicial system was not my consideration.

I envisioned the goals of advocacy and psychological support as roughly separable in time and focus and proposed to offer an advocacy focused group in the immediate aftermath of a criminal death (Rynearson & Sinnema, 1999) and a separate psychological support group when the family member could begin to focus more on themselves and less on the events of the crime. Advocacy was a service for family members after a criminal death (homicide, vehicular homicide, or accidental death), but the psychological support group was a service that could include family members after a suicidal death as well.

I envisioned a long-term, community project that provided service and a naturalistic study of family adjustment after a violent death. I anticipated identifying highly distressed family members within months of the violent death to prevent long term maladjustment.

In 1988 I held a series of community meetings that included represen-
tatives from the police, prosecuting attorneys, medical examiners, victim's
services, volunteer clergy, support groups, mental health centers, crisis
clinics, and crime victims compensation to enlist their cooperation in developing a community-based support program for family members after a
violent death. With their agreement and involvement, in 1989 we initiated The Support Project for Unnatural Dying.

Through the medical examiner's records, we have contacted and worked
with over a thousand family members after a violent death over the last
ten years. While this number sounds impressively large, it represents a
tiny fraction (less than 10%) of those family members who were eligible
for assistance. Those who asked for help wanted guidance with their
victim's compensation claims or advocacy with the media and the courts;
a much smaller number asked for direct psychological services because of
their high level of distress.

Like other clinical researchers who have committed themselves to a
long-term, prospective study of family members after a violent death, we
have been frustrated in overcoming the avoidance of families in the first
year after the death. While families we contact are grateful for our concern, not many are interested in our offer of support. Their avoidance
may be best for them, but is frustrating to me as a researcher, because it
keeps me from understanding how they remain resilient—and I am as
interested in defining how they successfully cope as I am in offering intervention when they cannot.

The family members who enroll in our program go through a semi-
structured interview to assess their resilience, their level of distress, and
their immediate needs. It is only after they have been stabilized, and we
have interviewed their family, that we consider how and when to intervene. If they are highly distressed and agree to commit themselves to a
time-limited group intervention, they complete a series of baseline tests.
Each group member completes a battery of standardized, self-report measures to screen for comorbid disorders of depression, trauma, substance
abuse, and traumatic grief before the group begins (see Appendix). These
measures are repeated at the end of the intervention to document change.
We have published several clinical papers that verify the intense and persistent trauma and grief distress in family members who have asked for
help (Rynearson, 1984; Rynearson & McCreary, 1993) and we are now
gathering outcome data to monitor the efficacy of our interventions.

Our project has developed and written manuals for two structured,
time-limited support groups—an advocacy group (**Criminal Death Support Group**) and a psychological reprocessing group (**Restorative Retelling Group**). Each group lasts for two hours, once a week for a total of

ten sessions. The group is limited to ten members and is closed to new members. Members may repeat the group if they need continued advocacy (because of ongoing investigation or trial) or if they remain highly distressed (because of persistent trauma or separation distress). Family members after suicide have been included in the Restorative Retelling Group (a heterogeneous group that contains members distressed by homicidal, accidental, and suicidal dying), but are not considered for the Criminal Death Support intervention. An agenda for each intervention is included in the appendix.

There are several obvious advantages to these structured and time-limited groups:

1. The screening process protects highly traumatized, non-resilient family members from entering a group that would further traumatize them. It also guides the clinician's identification of comorbid disorders that require a separate intervention.
2. With a structured, time-limited program, the family member is given a clear working model and agenda of the group and a goal to be reached in a defined interval of time. This can be very reassuring at times of distress. Members are told, *"Before we start the group, I want you to understand what we will be talking about and how this is going to help you in ten weeks."*
3. A short-term group does not allow members to become absorbed in problems beyond the effects of the violent death. Members are told, *"We are here to help you through the crisis of the violent dying, which is not to ignore other traumas—but we can't give you the time and attention that these traumas require—so let's arrange for someone else to help you with that problem outside of this group."*
4. Members join the group knowing there is a clear beginning and middle and closing to an intervention that is not an ending but a beginning— that their restoration is launched rather than finished by these groups, and that the group may be repeated.

These specialized interventions may be combined with concurrent individual or group therapies, and may be followed by a longer-term support group that meets less frequently for ongoing moderation of distress.

The agenda and format of either intervention is a way of reframing rather than a rigid framework to be compulsively followed. The group needs its own freedom in forming and finding its own balance. However, observing the order of the sessions is important. They proceed from early sessions that reinforce resilience and cohesion, to sessions that clarify confusion (criminal judicial orientation or models of distress), to sessions that re-expose each member to the stressor (actual court appearance, including impact statement or imagery of commemoration and dying), to final sessions that consolidate changes (family reinforcement and ritual farewell).

☐ Individual Intervention for Restorative Retelling

It is difficult for a solo clinician to start a support group for family members after a violent death because of the scarcity of violent dying. It is also unnatural for many family members to consider a group as potentially supportive. They prefer individual support. Though individual therapy is the most common intervention, there have been no studies that have tested its effectiveness with family members after a violent death. Very few clinicians have received training that prepares them for the specific effects and management of bereavement following violent dying, so they presumably support the family member through a confiding relationship and a safe setting for retelling, without a structured processing of the effects specific to grieving the violent death of a loved one. Enough resilience is reestablished with the support of a confiding relationship and safety that restoration can begin without additional attention. However, at the Support Project for Unnatural Dying we have treated nonresilient family members who were either self-referred or referred by their individual therapists because non-specific individual supportive therapy was ineffective. Had they focused their individual intervention more on the effects of trauma distress and restoration, the intervention may have been more successful.

The framework of restorative retelling can serve as a time-limited agenda in individual support, as well as in a group. Our project has developed a manual that presents restorative retelling as an individual intervention. The individual intervention follows a screening process and agenda very similar to the group intervention for restorative retelling. Individual sessions last for only one hour and begin with a session that reinforces resilience, then a session to clarify the goals of restoration, followed by sessions of commemoration and death imagery (re-exposure) and final sessions that reinforce meaning and reengagement. While this individual intervention lacks the dynamic advantages of a group (universality, altruism, vicarious learning and cohesiveness) it is more applicable and may be as effective. As a time-limited intervention it offers the same advantages of clear goals and termination often preferred by participants.

Agenda for Individual Intervention

Structured Interview and Screening Measures followed by:

Session 1:   Resilience — definition and skill enhancement
Session 2:   Key Concepts — definitions of trauma and separation
            distress
            1. Restorative retelling (model and goals)
            2. Preparation for commemoration
Session 3:   Life story of the deceased (pictures, writings, videos, etc.)
Session 4:   Relationship with the deceased (beginning, middle, and
            end)
            1. Concept of death (self and deceased)
            2. Concept of spirituality? (meaning)
            3. Preparation for death imagery
Session 5:   Review Death Imagery Drawing restorative introductions
            (rescue, reunion, and relinquish)
Session 6:   Relationship with dying memory
            1. Prevailing vs. recovery or retaliation
            2. Living and reengagement vs. disintegration
Session 7:   Meaning and reengagement
            1. Writings, drawings and readings
            2. Resources for vitality
Session 8:   Family Meeting consolidate and reinforce retelling
Session 9:   Ritual of Reconnection (continual commemoration) —
            may include family
Session 10: Termination
            1. Ongoing "agenda" for restorative retelling
            2. Repeat and compare screening measures (outcome)

This agenda cannot be presented as a protocol that has verified effectiveness. We cannot know if and how each of these topics and their assignment contributes to improvement. However, this condensed ordering of the sessions illustrates a form and structure that is similar to every short-term intervention for trauma distress. Restorative retelling may be specific in its key concepts and techniques, but its structure corresponds with an intuitive patterning and ordering inherent to time-limited trauma treatments.

Time-limited trauma interventions are focused on the effects of a specific external stressor (physical or sexual abuse, natural or human-induced disaster, criminal assault or violent death) and the limitation of time demands the use and staging of at least two techniques:

1. The moderation of distress (through a confiding relationship and a safe setting).
2. Re-exposure to the stressor (through a rational scheme that explains symptoms and an active procedure that restores health).

Restorative retelling, like every time-limited trauma intervention, begins with sessions that focus on reestablishing a sense of safety (resilience enhancement and stress reduction), followed by sessions that clarify an explanatory scheme (key concepts), and then sessions that focus on re-exposure (an active procedure for restoring through both commemoration and death imagery). The additional stressor of death includes the processing of separation distress (relationship with the deceased) as a simultaneous goal.

Perhaps the dynamic interplay of distress moderation and active re-exposure is more predictive of successful trauma treatment than any specific technique or strategy. If that is true, clinicians who do not include distress moderation and re-exposure to counterbalance the avoidance and intrusion of violent dying are probably ignoring a crucial therapeutic ingredient. Highly traumatized individuals in treatment cannot be expected to show progress unless and until they are engaged in a plan to relieve their distress while reliving their memory of what happened. The clinician misguides treatment by passively waiting for the patient to relive and revitalize spontaneously, or by insisting that that there is some unresolved conflict from the past. There may be underlying traumas or unconscious conflicts, but for someone acutely traumatized, these are irrelevant. No one acutely traumatized has the energy or concentration to begin that sort of complicated work. It is enough to help the person accommodate to this unspeakable event.

☐ Extension of Specialized Interventions

In 1997, through a grant from the Department of Justice's Office for Victims of Crime, we created a more specialized program, the Homicide Support Project, to serve family members victimized by homicide. The grant funds clinical training to replicate our Seattle program in other sites. Since 1997, we have trained teams of clinicians in several U.S. cities to apply our process of screening and focused, short-term group interventions. These and additional sites now form a cooperative matrix for a multi-site outcome study to monitor our effectiveness. Maintaining an affiliation between sites also encourages ongoing consultation and periodic retraining.

☐ Evidence of Effectiveness

While our specialized interventions are well described and replicated by other clinicians, our multi-site outcome study will take several years to complete. We anticipate our study will demonstrate restorative effects on family members, but those findings cannot prove that our intervention is necessarily responsible for the measurable changes. The design of our study does not allow a comparison of similar family members who complete our measures but who are not treated—a so-called control group. Such a study would verify that there was not only a measurable improvement with a 10-session intervention, but the change was caused by our treatment because the control group would show insignificant improvement in comparative scores. That sort of rigorous research design is beyond the reach of our community-based support project. We are responsible for providing immediate service to everyone who asks for help. Our primary purpose is clinical rather than research, so we cannot place family members in control groups.

There has been only one well-designed research study on the effects of intervention on adults after violent dying, and the results are promising (Murphy, 1998). Dr. Shirley Murphy and her colleagues in the School of Nursing at the University of Washington, carried out a longitudinal study of parents of children who had died violently (homicide, suicide, or accident). Through the medical examiner's records, the study contacted parents within a month of the child's violent death and requested their participation. Two hundred sixty one parents (62% of the total sample) agreed to join. They were randomly assigned to a nonintervention control group (70 mothers and 38 fathers) or a 10-session support group (101 mothers and 52 fathers). Measures of trauma, grief, physical health, marital strain, and mental distress were gathered before, after, and repeated at six months following a time-limited group intervention. This was an ambitious study with an unusually large number of subjects from a community sample rather than a clinic.

Each intervention group consisted of 5 to 10 members that met for ten 2-hour sessions. In the first hour the group leaders gave an informative presentation on an agenda of topics (trauma, grief, health, parental role loss, legal concerns, marital strain, family relationships, feelings toward others, expectations for the future). The second hour was a supportive group interaction to discuss the emotional impact of the death—and for members to receive emotional support. This agenda demonstrates that the researchers were providing a combination of cognitive clarification (a clear scheme of relevant problems and their resolution) and moderation of distress (supportive retelling and emotional interchange).

Those parents who completed the intervention were grateful for the experience and showed improvement on scores of trauma, grief, and mental distress. Mothers were more responsive to intervention than fathers, and those in the intervention group showed a significant treatment effect when compared with mothers who were in the control group. Parents of children killed by homicide were significantly more traumatized than parents accommodating to a suicide or accident. There were very few subjects who dropped out of the intervention or control group. Since these parents were gathered from a community sample rather than a clinic, they may have been more resilient and less comorbid than parents gathered from a clinic population.

This study (which continues to gather data after a five-year follow-up) is an objective verification of the efficacy of time-limited, focused group intervention with family members following violent death. The results validate what clinicians have long reported—that short-term, focused treatment can bring substantial relief to family members motivated to change. The study does not specify which ingredient of the intervention was most beneficial. Perhaps the opportunity for the telling and retelling of the dying story during the last hour of each session was more restorative than the first hour of information and discussion. While these results reassure us that intervention works, they cannot explain how or why.

☐ Guidance about Intervention

When someone asks for my professional judgment about treatment, I begin with an admission that there are no constants to guide us in knowing when or how to intervene. With that introduction, I try to open us to a high level of ambiguity and uncertainty in defining what might be helpful. The following are some common questions regarding treatment, along with my answers.

"What kind of treatment will help me?"

There are different treatments to choose from. Whether you decide on a peer support group or treatment with a clinician in group or individual therapy, you need to deal with the effects of violent dying. Don't start or remain in a treatment that is indefinite in duration or doesn't actively help you deal with the dying.

"How should I start treatment?"

It is wisest to begin with a review and reinforcement of your strengths and adaptive skills and a clear idea of what changes you want to make in yourself. An experi-

*enced clinician needs to help you in that assessment, and he or she can also diag-
nose disorders beyond the distress of the death that might respond to medication.
Treatment should begin with a thorough review of resilience and risks. Beware the
clinician who rushes into your retelling without getting to know you as a person.*

"How long is treatment?"

*You should feel some improvement after ten or twelve sessions. At that point you
and your clinician can decide if you are ready to continue restoring yourself on
your own.*

"How will I know that I am better?"

*You will be able to remember your loved one without being frightened and pos-
sessed with immediate thoughts of reenactment, remorse, retaliation, or protection.
You will feel closer to your memory of his or her living and detached from your
memory of his or her dying.*

"Will I ever be the same again?"

*Yes and no. In time the dying memory recedes, but when you think of the dying—
you can't be who you were before it. Treatment can't cure you by removing or
reversing its reality. The challenge is to continue your living around and through
the memory of the dying that remains, without it dominating your thinking or
sapping your vitality. The chances are very good that you can do that.*

Retelling the Literature on Violent Dying

As I have emphasized throughout the book, I am more intent on clarifying a restorative way of retelling violent dying than defining a specific theory. Because of its absolute incoherence, violent dying cannot be theorized. I have pointed to several secondary effects of violent dying (narrative incoherence, disintegrating trauma distress, identification with the last moments of the deceased, incomplete processing of the traumatic memory), but I have not sought a unifying theory. My model of retelling encourages each individual to change himself or herself in the process of retelling. That sort of transformative change is so subjective and unique that it cannot be proved or disproved by a single theory or protocol. Because my model is not based upon a firm theory, I have presented the practice of restorative retelling before its theoretical referents.

Instead of reviewing the literature on violent dying to synthesize a unifying theory, I include works that have served as a foundation for restorative retelling. My retelling of this literature is different than an exhaustive review. Many studies could be cited. While reiterating that list is informative, many of the citations are repetitious, without much substance, or of limited relevance to restorative retelling. Rather than a recital, my own review is selective—a gathering of several authors who have introduced guiding themes to restorative retelling. Retelling their chronology shows how their insights were introduced and integrated with one another.

If the beginning of this book was to appreciate the larger view of violent death as a tapestry, and the middle to separate some of the underlying patterns from one another, this chapter follows the colors and designs of several of the original workers.

☐ Historical Origins and Development: Freud and Janet

Only two psychiatric theorists published on death and trauma at the turn of the nineteenth century, but neither dealt with the combined effects of grief and trauma with violent dying. Sigmund Freud (1856–1939) was the first to develop a dynamic, explanatory model specific for death, and Pierre Janet (1859–1947) wrote extensively on the theory and treatment of trauma.

These two innovative thinkers met and studied traumatized patients together, but hardly acknowledged the work or insights of the other. Janet was a pupil and then associate of Jean Martin Charcot (1825–1893) the director of the Salpetriere, a Paris hospital that specialized in patients with neurological disorders. Freud studied there from October 1895 to February 1896 with Charcot and Janet. Presumably both Janet and Freud were deeply influenced by Charcot's clinical brilliance and his techniques of hypnosis. It was Charcot's dramatic treatment of patients with hysterical neurological reactions with hypnosis and his proposal that these hysterical reactions were associated with psychic trauma that propelled Janet and Freud to expand Chacot's psychological speculation.

Janet wrote extensively on trauma and theorized that when subjects experienced unbearable emotion associated with helplessness and terror, they were unable to process the memory of the event. Instead, the provocative memory and feeling was "dissociated"—rendered psychologically nonexistent. In his model, he proposed a direct correlation between dissociation and the degree of inescapable terror. In the clinical treatment of traumatized patients he established that it was not enough to simply express the feeling of terror. The patient also needed to become consciously aware and accepting of the memory of the trauma by overcoming avoidance and re-exposing themselves to the memory that had been so traumatic (Van der Kolk, 1989).

Freud accepted this same trauma dynamic during his early writings, viewing dissociation as a direct response to an external event, but he later proposed a trauma dynamic that was considerably more complex. He no longer accepted a direct causation between an external trauma and dissociation, but insisted on an underlying unconscious conflict as an intervening mechanism for dissociation. Finally, he considered dissociation to be primarily caused by repressed sexual or hostile feelings, which, in turn, were derivatives of early life traumas or repressed wishes. The treatment corollary of this model suggested that traumatized patients needed to remember and accept traumatic memories from their childhood interaction within their primary family—a much more ambitious treatment goal than Janet's.

In 1917 Freud wrote a paper entitled *Mourning and Melancholia* (Freud, 1957). In this very brief paper, he proposed that unconscious, conflicted feelings caused melancholia (pathologic grief). Melancholia was distinguished from mourning by symptoms of severe guilt, self-loathing, and suicidal thoughts that Freud explained as an unconscious directing of anger at the self. This was a natural extension of his complex model of trauma—that death was "traumatic" because there were irresolvable sexual or aggressive conflicts with the memory of the deceased—and pathologic grief should be treated through an analysis of those repressed complexes of feelings.

Much later he postulated that death was an "instinct," an inborn drive to die—which never achieved clinical equivalence with the sexual drive in his theory. His concept of the death instinct remained a puzzling addition that was never fully integrated into his theory and had even less relevance to treatment. Instead, it was this earlier speculation on the relationship between unconscious conflict and prolonged grief that had an enormous effect on generations of clinicians.

These two models of trauma and grief continued as guiding principles for subsequent theorists and clinicians during the early decades of the twentieth century. Janet's adherents did not find in his model the wide and sometimes misleading extensions of application and treatment promised in Freudian psychoanalysis. Janet's working model was parsimonious and focused on the abnormal processing of traumatic memory without the highly speculative formulations of unconscious conflict.

Both of these theoreticians wrote and practiced in a time of extreme intellectual ferment. Each included vivid metaphors as a basis for their models, and, of course, there was no way of refuting what they proposed. Their theories were based on their ingenious speculations rather than rigorous measurement of objective data. At that time, the power and universality of theory corresponded with the power and the universality of metaphors and narratives retold as theory—particularly with Freud who, as a classical scholar, based many of his narrative models on Greek myths (specifically, Oedipus, Electra, and Narcissus) that lent drama to his model of unconscious conflict. The other major theorists of the era (Jung, Adler, Rank, Deutsch, and Abraham) were just as powerful in embellishing their own narrative insights, but none added enduring themes specific to trauma and grief.

Freud's more convoluted and unconscious models gradually eclipsed the others, including Janet's simpler model of trauma. The Freudian speculations on the significance of the unconscious extended far beyond clinical practice and pervaded the art, literature, and social thought of the 1920s and '30s. And no wonder, for it not only contained some measure of truth and therapeutic promise, but also drew its source of energy from a metaphysical and mythical wellspring. It is not surprising that Freud's model of the unconscious biased the observations of clinicians for many decades.

☐ The Original Study of Violent Death: The Cocoanut Grove Disaster

Certainly when 491 people die in a fire, the event presents an overwhelming combination of trauma and grief—not one, but both. The public narrative of this fire is retold in enough detail to show a missed opportunity in integrating the original insights of Janet and Freud. The clinicians who treated the survivors of the Cocoanut Grove fire (Dr. Alexandra Adler and Dr. Eric Lindemann) wrote separate papers that perpetuated the divergence of these two models for another forty years.

The story began in a nightclub, The Cocoanut Grove, in downtown Boston, MA, that was filled with nearly 1,000 partygoers on a November night in 1942. "Packed" would be more accurate, in describing the massing of revelers in a multilevel building of only 11,000 square feet. Holy Cross had won their football game that afternoon and there was a contingent of celebrants loudly toasting their victory. Boston was preparing for war, so there were many service personnel there as well, including hospital workers. Burn units had been established at Massachusetts General and Boston City Hospitals in the event of a naval attack and massive fire.

The fire began in a decorated light fixture in the basement and roared upward through the building. There were no emergency exits, only a door to the kitchen, and the revolving door at the front of the building that jammed. There was no way out. Nothing could have saved the hundreds who died at the scene. Without any ventilation or exits, it was remarkable that anyone survived the wall of superheated gasses that pushed before the fire. Those who died at the scene immediately suffocated from acute pulmonary burns and edema.

It was a celebration turned nightmare. Vivid accounts from survivors described the terror-stricken screams that filled the rooms of total darkness, and the desperate lunging through doors and stairways that promised escape—only to be thrown aside or crushed by others. Some saved themselves by crawling beneath tables where they found enough air to survive.

A fleet of taxis and ambulances rushed the casualties to every emergency facility in the Boston area. Boston City Hospital and Massachusetts General Hospital received most of the burn cases. Cases were triaged, and the dead and dying overflowed the hallways into the hospital grounds. An emergency morgue was set up in a nearby building where lines of relatives tried to identify their family members from the long rows of bodies.

Boston City admitted more survivors (131) than Massachusetts General (39). The surgery and medical staffs (including neuropsychiatry) followed protocols they had established for war-related disaster. Within the first two weeks their primary task was to provide physical stabilization for the skin and pulmonary burns. There was a high death rate—about 25% of those admitted died from their burns—and by the time neuropsychiatry assessed the remainder, many of the survivors had been discharged.

Psychiatric evaluation was completed on 54 survivors at Boston City, and 17 survivors at Massachusetts General. Dr. Alexandra Adler at Boston City and Dr. Eric Lindemann at Massachusetts General carried out independent studies on the psychiatric effects of the violent dying on survivors. Both studied survivors from the same event, but their separate explanations of their findings could not have been more divergent.

Adler's study (1943) highlighted what she termed, "post traumatic mental complications" and included a nine-month follow-up assessment of 46 of the 54 survivors. Dr. Adler did not recommend psychological treatment for anyone in her study. Lindemann's study narrowly focused on what he called "pathologic grief." In his detailed observations of 7 survivors, he assessed and treated them with techniques of "crisis intervention."

The bias of their observations and explanations is illustrated in their narrative reports of two survivors. Both of these young men survived the fire after attempting to rescue their wives who died at the scene. It is remarkable to see how each author's preconceived model of violent death (Adler's singular model of trauma and Lindemann's exclusive model of grief) distort the author's observations and interpretations of nearly identical cases from the same event.

Adler's Narrative Case

A youth of 20, a clerk, had been somewhat excitable and easily angered prior to his injury but aside from that had been well adjusted to his professional and married life. On the night of the disaster he was about to leave the nightclub and stood near an exit waiting for his wife, who was four months pregnant. He suddenly saw flames, was milled around, lost sight of his wife and soon escaped through an exit. The patient suffered second degree burns of the face, neck and hands. Five percent of the total skin area was involved. Shortly before leaving the hospital he was told by the priest that his wife had perished in the fire. Until then he had thought that she had been saved. He became deeply depressed and has been so ever since. He went back to work but his working capacity has suffered. He is much slower and has lost all interest in his work. In his spare time he thinks of the disaster and of his wife, feels that he will never be interested in another girl. He cannot concentrate and starts to shake all over whenever he has a slight argument. He is constantly afraid of another fire and would never dare to go to a nightclub again. He sits down in moving pictures only if there is a seat in the last row, so that he can get out quickly. He takes the same precautions in dining rooms. The sound of fire engines awakens him at night with a start. He had not had nightmares in the hospital, but they began one week after he came home. In the following months he relived the scenes of the fire in five terrifying dreams. They still occur, though rarely. The patient was rejected by the army in March 1943 with the diagnosis of psychoneurosis. This depresses him deeply because he had hoped to be able to forget through strenuous army life. He is trying again to join the Army and intends to join the Merchant Marine if again rejected. (Adler, 1943, p. 1100)

This report illustrates that grief was not considered to be of much significance in survivors evaluated by Dr. Adler. Her study documented that one half of the survivors who were unrecovered at nine months had not experienced the death of a relative or close friend in the fire, suggesting that grief was not a significant stressor as compared with the direct effects of the disaster. Instead, she viewed the intrusive and avoidant responses to the trauma of the disaster as disabling. Further, she viewed these effects as biological instead of psychological, and she predicted spontaneous improvement with time. Her study did not contain any treatment recommendations.

This was the only paper that she wrote on this topic. Adler's study did not catalyze much enthusiasm or interest. Despite her assessment of three times as many survivors and a more rigorous protocol of measurement and follow-up, her paper was virtually disregarded.

Lindemann's Narrative Case

A young man aged 32 had received only minor burns and left the hospital apparently well on the road to recovery just before the psychiatric survey of the disaster victims took place. On the fifth day he had learned that his wife had died. He seemed somewhat relieved of his worry about her fate; impressed the surgeon as being unusually well controlled during the following short period of his stay in the hospital. On January 1st he was returned to the hospital by his family. Shortly after his return home he had become restless, did not want to stay at home, had taken a trip to relatives trying to find rest, had not succeeded, and had returned home in a state of marked agitation, appearing preoccupied, frightened and unable to concentrate on any organized activity.

He would try to start conversations, break them off abruptly, and then fall into repeated murmured utterances: "Nobody can help me. When is it going to happen? I am doomed, am I not?"

With intense morbid guilt feelings, he reviewed incessantly the events of the fire. His wife had stayed behind. When he tried to pull her out, he had fainted and was shoved out by the crowd. She was burned alive while he was saved. "I should have saved her or I should have died too." He complained about being filled with an incredible violence and did not know what to do about it. The rapport established with him lasted for only brief periods of time. He then would fall back into his state of intense agitation and muttering. He slept poorly even with large sedation. In the course of four days he became somewhat more composed, had longer periods of contact with the psychiatrist, and seemed to feel that he was being understood and might be able to cope with his morbid feelings of guilt and violent impulses. On the sixth day of his hospital stay, however, after skillfully distracting the attention of his special nurse, he jumped through a closed window to a violent death. (Lindemann, 1944, p. 146)

There is no question that this young man was presenting with a more intense depression (presumably a psychotic depression) than the young man cited in Adler's study, and ended his life in the drama of his own violent death. However, Lindemann's retrospective reporting of the failed treatment and his repeated references to "morbid guilt" and "being filled with an incredible violence" are echoes of Freud's theory of pathologic grief. Lindemann suggests that the patient killed himself because of his repressed, self-directed anger—not because of the traumatic image of his wife being burned alive. He disregarded the horrific imagery that this young man most probably experienced, and failed to acknowledge the direct effects of the helplessness and terror forced upon him by the fire.

Grief, not trauma, was the critical variable in Lindemann's assessment of the seven survivors whom he actively followed and treated, and there was no comparative follow-up in survivors who were untreated. He was so convinced of the causal linkage between pathologic grief and repressed feelings (Freud's model) that he insisted on the clinical necessity of rapidly releasing these repressed feelings with eight or ten individual therapy sessions. His view of acute grief as a "crisis" responsive to time-limited, focused psychotherapy was probably effective for some, but not all, of the survivors. Perhaps the intense preparedness for war in 1942 galvanized crisis therapy as imperative. Lindemann recognized that he was preparing clinicians who would probably be involved with wartime deaths, and he may have been over-determined to outline a practical approach.

Lindemann's initial study led to an expanded paper in the next year

(Lindemann, 1944), based upon 101 survivors of violent death—the 17 subjects from the Cocoanut Grove fire, and the remainder from his out-patient and inpatient practice. It was this second paper that identified Lindemann as an authority through his expanded definition and treatment of pathologic grief. It is intriguing that both of his papers are based upon clinical findings from survivors of violent death, but their traumatic distress isn't recognized or included in his interpretation.

He continued to write and lecture extensively on the topic of grief and its treatment. His strident recommendation that survivors be encouraged to express their repressed feelings of sadness and anger became axiomatic in clinical treatment.

Nearly 20 years ago, I tried to understand all that I could about the Cocoanut Grove fire, because every theoretician who writes about grief makes reference to the psychological studies of its survivors. When I tried to contact the original investigators, I found that Dr. Lindemann was de-ceased, but Dr. Adler was living in New York. We corresponded and I met with her on several occasions. My first questions dealt with the diver-gence of their reports: Did she and Dr. Lindemann communicate with each other after the fire? Or consider a combined study? Or present their findings to one another?

She had tried to talk with Dr. Lindemann, but was rebuffed. According to Dr. Adler, who was the daughter of Alfred Adler (one of Freud's associ-ates in Vienna), Dr. Lindemann did not respect her "Adlerian" views, and there were also boundary issues because of the competition between the two academic teaching centers. Personal and political factors apparently forced them to carry out separate studies. While she respected Dr. Lindemann as a clinician, she was not "enchanted" (her word) with his Freudian theory of the unconscious. Like her father, she felt Freud's pre-occupation with unconscious anger and sexuality was erroneous, and she couldn't understand why his theory was so popular in America. Though she did not cite Janet in her paper, she recognized his model, which formed the basis of her understanding of the trauma of the fire.

Retelling these details of the Cocoanut Grove fire and two of its inves-tigators illustrates the clashing of narrative models through the meta-phors of the body (the physiology of trauma) or the mind (the psychol-ogy of the unconscious). Unfortunately, this same false theoretical dichotomy continues, as does institutional territoriality, and I have won-dered how the Cocoanut Grove fire survivors would be assessed and treated now—almost sixty years later—in Boston or any other major city. I will return to that question in the next chapter, but at this point my review shows the historical and clinical resistances to integrating the models of trauma and separation. Even when the Cocoanut Grove fire provided an abundant opportunity, Adler and Lindemann were more intent on defending and promoting their own model than cooperatively blending their insights into a comprehensive understanding of violent death—an unfortunate legacy of the egotism and insularity of Janet and Freud.

☐ War and Genocide: Frankl, Krystal, and Lifton

World War I was followed by a modest number of psychological reports describing the traumatic effects of combat and death exposure on young soldiers. It was enough to describe the traumatic reactions of amnesia, acute psychosis, terror, and avoidance—all subsumed under the diagnosis of "shell shock." There was no need for theory to explain why these soldiers responded in such a highly dysfunctional way beyond their inability to adjust to their persistent terror and exposure to violent death while trapped in trenches, overcome by clouds of mustard gas, and showered by bullets and shrapnel and desperate bayonet attacks. It was too obvious and intuitive—those who lacked "character" could not cope. General physicians serving in the military, had little familiarity with psychiatry and offered non-specific therapeutic measures—rest, sedatives, hypnosis, and hydrotherapy.

World War II occurred at a time when psychiatry had become a valid subspecialty, practiced with out-patients as well as in-patients, and the public and medical community accepted it as relevant. Every branch of the military had psychiatric services for its personnel and their treatments were specific and innovative. Military psychiatrists began to use techniques of re-exposure, group therapy, and community psychiatry to aid in the recovery of highly traumatized personnel, but there were few original or innovative theories cited in their reports.

Perhaps the ubiquity of violent dying with war does not require a specific theory or explanation of its effects. In war, the inevitability of violent dying makes it expected and acceptable—a risk rather than an abhorrent act. After all, slaying the enemy is the final purpose, and soldiers are valued for their bravery in killing. Combatants are indoctrinated to kill without question, and dying in battle is retold as heroic. Even when killed, soldiers are not viewed as victims, for no one actively fighting in a war is seen as innocent. If they fight, they are "fair game" for dying violently.

Presumably the high expectancy and impersonality of violent death during war makes it more coherent than the violent death of a family member from homicide, suicide, or accident. While military personnel directly exposed to violent death during combat are at risk for being traumatized, only a minority become disabled by the effects of witnessing or perpetrating violent death, and those who remain impaired present with high comorbidity, particularly substance abuse (Kulka et al., 1990).

It is rare that the violent dying of warfare is deemed criminal or followed by an investigation or trial—unless the killing involves innocent civilians or noncombatants. This absence of a social inquest and assignment of blame and punishment further differentiates violent dying in a military conflict from violent dying in a public community.

World War II, like any other major war, involved the violent deaths of millions of innocent civilians. Violent death of noncombatants always accompanies war, and its effects on the community of survivors or surviving family members is complicated by its unwarranted cruelty. Noncombatants should not be fair game. If there can be anything lawful about war, it should reserve killing for active adversaries.

The Holocaust and the bombing of Hiroshima were two atrocities of genocide during World War II that were particularly egregious. Such acts of genocide are distinguished from other forms of violent dying by the massive targeting and deliberate obliteration of an entire group of people justified by an idealized goal—the psychotic ideal of supremacy and "cleansing," or the enforced ideal of sacrificing an entire city to nuclear devastation to ensure victory.

Unlike the Cocoanut Grove disaster, the survivors of the Holocaust and Hiroshima were intentionally forced to remain immersed in grotesque dying for days, weeks, months, or even years. Several researchers focused on the specific effects of the genocide on these noncombatants in systematic clinical studies—the first clinical studies to recognize the unique clinical effects of violent dying. Violent death was so pervasive that each survivor anticipated his or her own violent dying, and the researchers, like the survivors, were absorbed by the enormity of the killing. Clinical investigators of the Holocaust (Frankl, 1959; Krystal, 1968) and Hiroshima (Lifton, 1968) focused on the direct effects of the violent dying on survivors, rather than the physiological effects of trauma or the unconscious dynamics of grief as Adler and Lindemann had done with the Cocoanut Grove fire. These early reports of Frankl, Krystal, and Lifton are highlighted because the originality of their insights has formed the basis for our theoretical understanding of traumatic bereavement after violent death.

Viktor Frankl was a psychiatrist before he was imprisoned in a concentration camp during World War II. His slim volume *From Death Camp to Existentialism* (1959), first published in Germany in 1946, contains the narrative account of his own incarceration. He lost everything, including his wife and virtually all of his relatives. In ninety-three pages, in the voice of participant-observer and psychiatrist, he outlines the responses of terror and helplessness associated with violent dying. In the first few days he and others noted outcries of despair and then shock, replaced by an intense longing for home and family, and a final response of "depersonalization"—so one could exist, but not react. Those who could find no hope or purpose in this death immersion passively surrendered, withdrew, and died. For Frankl and others who survived, he noted a capacity of resilient survivors to make a fundamental change in their attitude toward life.

> We had to learn ourselves, and furthermore we had to teach the despairing men, that it did not really matter what we expected from life, but what life expected from us. We needed to stop asking about the meaning of life and instead to think of ourselves as those who were being questioned by life—daily and hourly. Our answer must consist, not in talk or meditation, but in right action and in right conduct.
> (Frankl, 1959, p.77)

Frankl found autonomy from imminent dying by actively engaging with others and finding meaning in a momentary act that offered some purpose and future goal. This transcendent attitude, and the purposeful engagement that followed, served as an experiential foundation for what he called logotherapy, a psychotherapy based upon the will to find meaning, that he maintained was the most essential human drive of all. Value was placed on the attitudinal responses to the triangulation of suffering, guilt, and death.

> Everything can be taken from man, but one thing, the last of the human freedoms, to choose one's attitude in any given situation, even if only for a few moments.
> (Frankl, 1962, p. 110)

For Frankl, despair was suffering minus meaning. In the face of unavoidable suffering, freely choosing a unique self-transcendent response was powerfully redeeming.

Henry Krystal was also a concentration camp survivor. He spent his adolescence in the camps, an experience that had a profound effect on his subsequent psychiatric practice and writing. In evaluating and treating survivors of the Holocaust he noted a common finding of emotional "numbing" that he viewed as a maladaptive response to the "catastrophic trauma" of the camps. His early model roughly corresponded to Janet's and proposed a mechanism of generalized adaptive failure in tolerating the affect of disintegratory terror. Instead of dissociation, he called the amnesia and disavowal "cataplectic passivity."

In understanding the effects of violent dying on survivors, Krystal's most enduring insight and theoretical construct was in regard to the inability of impaired survivors to comfort themselves (Krystal, 1978). In his model, he suggested that as traumatized survivors regressed in psychological functioning, there was a diminishment in their self-comforting functions. Without the capacity to calm themselves, they were unable to process experience in a stable and accurate manner. Consequently, they dealt with their high arousal by substance abuse or assuming a total detachment ("alexthymia") from feeling of any kind—pleasure or pain.

Krystal recommended that an early goal of therapy, for those who were this traumatized and incapable of moderating their feeling, was to restore their capacity for self-care through direct engagement and support. In later writings he elaborated this trauma model into a highly complex system that included other major psychiatric disorders, and a separate developmental model of trauma affect for children.

Robert Lifton studied survivors of the nuclear bombing of Hiroshima. He developed a model of human adaptation based upon the instinctive need for "formative" mental function—the process of creating viable inner forms. This capacity for creating generative symbols was crucial in compensating for the extreme absurdity and disintegration of the survivors' death imagery after witnessing the evaporation of their entire city. In this model, the obliterative death imagery overwhelmed the ongoing imagery of the continuity of life. With this distortion of formative imagery the survivor presented with a syndromal response—"psychic numbing," survivor guilt, suspicion of kindness or "counterfeit nurturance," and the struggle to reestablish formative inner symbols. In this circumstance of overwhelming stress, Lifton explicitly rejected Freud's model of the unconscious (though he was psychoanalytically trained himself) and instead drew upon the work of Erikson, Cassier, Langer, and Boulding and their writings on symbolization (Lifton, 1976, pp. 13–20).

Lifton worked directly with the survivors' death imagery in individual and group therapy, and later this same model was used with Vietnam veterans who had been traumatized as combatants. His therapeutic stance included advocacy and mutual participation in supporting the justified anger and need for retribution in his patients. He was an activist and spoke out against nuclear weapons and the Vietnam War.

These early writings of Frankl, Krystal, and Lifton—tentative and tightly focused on the direct effects of genocide on the survivor—are some of the earliest dynamic insights of violent dying and its treatment. Unlike Adler and Lindemann, these authors viewed violent dying as specifically associated with unbearable incoherence (Frankl), unbearable affect (Krystal), or unbearable imagery (Lifton). Their description and naming of responses were unique—"depersonalization" for Frankl, "numbing" for Krystal, or "psychic numbing" for Lifton—for what we now call avoidance. Lifton, more than the others, focused on the primacy of death imagery—what we now call intrusion—as an involuntary response to violent dying.

Their shared dynamic insights, theories, and therapeutic strategies for survivors after violent dying were fundamental. They were the first investigators who studied and clarified a dynamic understanding of the psychological effects of violent dying, and the last to present a dynamic theory to explain their findings.

☐ DSM I–IV and Dynamic Devaluation

The writings and the psychiatric teaching of the 1950s, '60s and '70s were the last decades that encouraged investigators to understand the dynamics of psychological problems. Beginning in the 1980s there was a dramatic shift from valuing psychodynamic theory and practice, to an insistence on an objective protocol by which psychiatric disorders could be reliably measured. The Diagnostic and Statistical Manual (e.g., DSM-IV; American Psychiatric Association, 1994) and its many revisions is the defining text of that model.

The DSM defines psychiatric disorders on the basis of observable signs and symptoms, in statistically significant clusters which, when lasting a specified time, meet the criteria of pattern and duration to warrant a valid diagnosis. That sentence is tedious because it describes a system whose sole (and soulless) purpose is descriptive of what can be externally observed rather than internally experienced. It arbitrarily dismisses consideration of loss (such as the death of a family member) as problematic unless that family member's bereavement (separately coded as a nonsignificant "relational" stressor) includes the signs and symptoms of a major psychiatric disorder (such as major depression).

There is no room in the DSM for consideration of how and when a family member's internal experience of violent dying is problematic. Indeed, there is no "problem" unless the person presents enough signs and symptoms over time to meet criteria for a comorbid but separate disorder such as Major Depression, Posttraumatic Stress Disorder or Substance Abuse.

Acute and chronic trauma distress maintains some legitimacy as a valid psychiatric disorder. After a violent death, if family members meet the criteria for Posttraumatic Stress Disorder, they are recognized by courts and insurance companies as having a medical condition that deserves retribution and payment for treatment. With no appearance of "Grief Disorder" in the DSM manual, grief does not.

Since the acceptance of the DSM model, the literature on violent dying has been swept by a wave of "objectivism." Unfortunately, in their zeal for measurement, current investigators have lost incentive to understand or explain their findings. The text of data-driven studies is filled with descriptions of methodology, measurement and presentation of results followed by a meager, concluding paragraph virtually empty of explanation.

With so much objective data and so little clarification, I occasionally pine for the certitude of earlier authors who knew what they were looking for, and could find it in the narrative case presentation of their patient. I wouldn't be fooled by their certitude, but I would at least be refreshed by their creative speculation – something in their own thinking, beyond the data.

This devaluation of the dynamic understanding of surviving violent dying is absurd. Surviving needs a dynamic model. The static approach of DSM ignores the guiding insights of original investigators and returns us to the relatively drab understanding of eighty or ninety years ago—when World War I soldiers who could not cope with violent dying were understood as lacking some undefined ingredient in their "character" or neurobiology.

Perhaps the DSM insistence on objectivity is a reaction against the unbridled, subjective speculations of past investigators. While some correction may be warranted, DSM-IV is an over-determined corrective for some disorders that are clearly reactive, and perpetuates the false dichotomy of objective versus subjective – a dichotomy that needs to be dispelled because both are crucial to clinical understanding. The DSM model has increased our diagnostic objectivity, but the DSM ideology of sacrificing subjective understanding for objective knowledge is spurious and misleading in understanding or helping someone after a violent dying.

☐ Current Research on Violent Dying

Since the 1980s, an increasing number of clinical researchers have focused more specifically on the effects of homicidal, suicidal, or accidental dying on family members. Unfortunately, that focus has become narrow and exclusive. Few of these authors make any reference to the historical work of the dynamic theorists we have just reviewed, or to the work of someone outside their specific category of violent dying. Instead of considering violent dying as a common cause of a common response, each type of violent dying is viewed as a separate clinical entity with its own literature. There is little basis for making that discrimination beyond the designation of the action of the killing. There are more similarities than differences between the response to a violent death from suicide, accident, homicide, natural or man-made disaster, warfare, or genocide. Whoever survives any type of violent death retells the way of the dying and accommodates to their trauma and separation distress as they try to find a restorative accommodation. Categorizing solely on the mode of violent dying ignores variables of the survivor (e.g., gender, kinship, degree of attachment, and caring) that may have a more significant impact than the way the person was killed.

Perhaps the clustering of surviving family members by the mode of dying is self-selective. Local support groups tend to form around the specific way that the person died. Members of Survivors of Suicide, Parents of Murdered Children, Mothers Against Drunk Driving and other peer-led support groups, can readily identify with one another by the way of violent dying. Researchers who gather samples also seek a homogeneous group for study and hesitate to simultaneously enroll family members whose loved ones experienced different types of violent death.

Since the clinical literature on the effects of violent death on survivors follows these same separable subgroups, my review traces their beginnings. At the outset, studies were purely descriptive of the subjective responses of patients who presented for treatment. Regardless of whether the dying was from a homicide, suicide, or accident, these authors noted similar responses of trauma distress and preoccupation with the criminal–judicial aftermath, though there were some subtle differences that could not be measured with standardized measures. Without standardized measures for cross-comparison, most of the investigations are descriptive and anecdotal.

The Survivors of Homicide

Homicide is the least frequent form of violent dying, yet has a profound impact on surviving family members. Since homicide often involves an intentional and transgressive act, homicide is followed by the strongest criminal–judicial response.

Dr. Ann Burgess, a psychodynamically trained investigator, was the first to publish a pilot study in 1975 describing the responses of nine family members after a homicidal dying (Burgess, 1975). Pioneering in her studies of women who had been raped, Dr. Burgess found a subgroup that had also been traumatized by the homicidal death of a family member. Her brief report of nine family members who presented for treatment lucidly outlines the intense terror, phobic avoidance, flashbacks and dreams of the dying, the intense stress and diversion of the criminal-judicial aftermath, and the long-term adjustment of the entire family to the tragedy. She named this response, "the homicide-trauma syndrome" and proposed an underlying dynamic of "victim-oriented thoughts" or preoccupying identification with the way the loved one died. There were no specific recommendations for treatment beyond immediate support with crisis counseling. Burgess's paper contained the essential descriptive features (trauma distress, criminal–judicial and community preoccupation, and long-term complications of grief).

Similar descriptions of the psychological effects of homicide have been expanded and buttressed by empirical studies of several authors (Amick-Mullen, Kilpatrich, Veronen, & Smith, 1989; Parkes, 1993; Rinear, 1988; Rynearson, 1984). However, these subsequent studies only corroborate what she first clarified. Her original observations have remained foundational.

Dr. Shirley Murphy's recent study (Murphy, 1999) of parental bereavement after violent dying has added objective verification to these clinical descriptions of intense acute and long-term distress, showing that homicidal dying is associated with higher distress than suicidal or accidental dying. This is the first study to document this difference, and its findings need to be verified by other naturalistic studies of violent dying.

The intense criminal–judicial aftermath of homicidal dying and its psychological negotiation by the family member is disorienting and frustrating. There have been two books (Redmond, 1989; Spungen, 1998) that offer definitions of legal terms and victims advocate services. It takes an entire book to begin unraveling the high complexity of this process.

The Survivors of Suicide

This mode of violent dying is more frequent than homicide and appears to present the surviving family member with the lonely dilemma of trying to explain the loved one's death. Though the dying was highly intentional, the murderer and the victim disappeared in the same act. There is no one to left to apprehend or punish.

Perhaps the most widely read book on suicide, *The Savage God,* was written by Alfred Alvarez in 1971 with an updated edition in 1990. It is a masterfully written sociocultural history of suicide and its effect on the arts and artists, including the author. At thirty-one, this English poet and essayist survived a near fatal suicide attempt, and he views the drive for self destruction as self-imposed, " . . . a terrible but utterly natural reaction to the strained, narrow, unnatural necessities we sometimes create for ourselves (Alvarez, 1990, p. 307)." He suggests that some great artists are impelled by an effort to give form to this nameless self-disintegration.

An enormous clinical literature exists regarding the treatment of someone who is suicidal, but very little regarding the effects of suicide on survivors. A recent literature review of the effects of suicide on bereavement included only seventy published papers (Ness & Pfeffer, 1990) that noted multiple reports of acute trauma responses with terror, avoidance, intrusive flashbacks, and dreams. A more unique finding on the effects of suicidal dying highlighted by the review was the intense stigma that complicated its acceptance and communication. Family members sometimes insisted that the death was accidental or homicidal because they could not tolerate the shame and disgrace associated with self-destruction. The stigma was reinforced by the virtual absence of an investigation by the police or court, or a community response of support and respect for the deceased. With suicide, more than any other form of violent dying, family members are isolated in searching for an explanation of the tragedy. The authors' review also suggested that these findings of trauma distress, social stigma, and avoidance last for many years, but there was little objective data beyond anecdotal reports to substantiate these differences.

Dr. Sue Chance, a psychiatrist and writer, wrote a powerful and insightful book (Chance, 1992) on the subjective experience of suicidal bereavement after her son's suicide. In this small volume, the author shares excerpts from a journal she kept that helped her reconstruct a narrative through the maze of confused thoughts and feelings that she retold herself in her writing. By the end of the book she has revealed herself as permanently changed, but resolute in her commitment to life and helping others as a way of saving herself from the despair of her son's decision to kill himself.

Survivors of Accidental Death

Accidental dying from motor vehicles is the most frequent form of violent dying. Surviving family members are at risk for acute and sustained psychological responses to the loss and anger at the criminal–judicial system.

Since dying in a motor vehicle accident is an expected risk (like the soldier dying in combat), it is more comprehensible than homicide or suicide, but nonetheless traumatic. The surviving family views the dying as particularly transgressive when the fatality occurs because of the other driver's negligence or inebriation, in which case the deceased is identified as a victim. When the other driver is clearly at fault, a criminal–judicial inquest follows, but it is decidedly less punitive than the inquest after an intentional homicide.

Family members were so enraged with the lack of criminal–judicial response to vehicular homicide that in the 1980s they began to organize themselves for collective support and protest. Mothers Against Drunk Driving (MADD) has been a remarkably vocal and effective organization in legislating a more preventive and punitive response to drunk driving and equivalent punishment and sentencing for vehicular homicide. Janice Lord was director of clinical services for MADD when she wrote *No Time for Goodbyes* (Lord, 1987) for family members after the accidental death of a loved one, as a concise and readable guide in clarifying trauma and grief distress, with pragmatic advice for dealing with the helplessness so often experienced in gaining justice and retribution.

There has been a recent review of the clinical studies of bereavement after accidental dying (Malt, 1994) verifying the intense responses of trauma and grief distress, with objective measures that document acute and sustained effects. These objective findings are not surprising or inconsistent with what has been clinically recognized.

The literature on accidental dying contains little, if any, theory to explain its findings of intense distress, beyond the suddenness of the dying and the inadequacy of retribution and punishment. Perhaps the relative lack of intent with accidental dying diminishes the imaginary reenactment—since the dying was not planned or purposeful, it does not require so much elaboration in retelling—and particularly so if the deceased was driving and was at fault for the accident.

☐ Traumatic Bereavement: A Blending of Trauma and Bereavement

The clinical literatures of trauma and bereavement have followed this same division since World War II, during which the studies of trauma and bereavement have matured, but grown in parallel. It will take time for this cleavage to mend.

During the 60s, 70s, and 80s, bereavement literature presented well-designed prospective studies (e.g., Bowlby, Parkes, Raphael, Jacobs, Zisook, and Schuchter) that demonstrated the frequency and trajectories of spousal bereavement responses and new theoretical insights – that bereavement is based upon interrupted attachment or the universal need for nurturance instead of an unconscious mechanism. There are excellent recent reviews of the theory and classification of grief (Jacobs, 1993) and its treatment (Rando, 1993) for the reader who seeks detailed information on the clinical effects of natural dying and its treatment.

At the same time clinicians who specialized in trauma carried out their own prospective studies on subjects traumatized by abuse (Foa & Rothbaum, 1998; Herman, 1992) war (Van der Kolk, 1996), or disasters (Green, Grace, & Lindy, 1990, McFarlane, Clayer, & Bookless, 1997) and emphasized the psycho-physiologic basis for sustained trauma responses. New strategies were developed that combined medication and focused cognitive therapies to stabilize and then reexpose subjects to their memory of the trauma (Foa, Keane, & Friedman, 2000; Meichenbaum, 1994).

Over this same period of time, several investigators (Figley, 1996a; Horowitz, 1976; Rando, 1993) conceptualized loss as not only associated with responses of bereavement, but with responses of trauma. Horowitz was the first to clarify this multidimensional view in basing his conceptual model of grief on the dynamic of trauma—that the loss of an emotionally valued person was a major stressor processed through alternating responses of intrusion and avoidance. He and his associates developed measures of trauma distress (Impact of Event Scale) and strategies of short-term individual treatment for family members who remained highly distressed following a death. However, there has been no consideration of violent dying in their work.

In the last five years a new literature has appeared that considers trauma and bereavement as coexistent responses after a death. This contains an exciting, new bridging of the conceptual division that began over a century ago with Freud and Janet. Drs. Prigerson and Jacobs (in press) clarified a reliable measure (Traumatic Inventory of Grief) of a syndrome of combined trauma and separation distress following death called Traumatic Grief. This syndrome is based upon their investigation of family members after natural dying, and is presumably based upon underlying attachment vulnerability. Without the nurturing presence of the deceased, someone with traumatic bereavement presents with intrusive and avoidant responses to the death. Dr. Shear (2001) has developed a short-term, individual treatment (Traumatic Grief Therapy) for Traumatic Grief that showed measurable effectiveness in a preliminary trial with ten patients after natural dying. These investigators, like Horowitz and his associates (Horowitz et al, 1997), do not consider the independent effects of violent dying on trauma distress.

☐ Summary

My review of the literature on violent dying reveals a wandering focus. It began with the incisive speculations of Janet and Freud on trauma and grief, with their conflicting narrative models of external and unconscious conflict. This misguiding and divisive focus was perpetuated by the early investigators of violent dying in the Cocoanut Grove fire aftermath (Adler and Lindemann), but was narrowed to the more specific effects of violent dying in studying the survivors of genocide after World War II. That literature clarified the overwhelming effect of genocide on meaning (Frankl), feeling (Krystal), and cognition (Lifton) that form the basis of our understanding of the psychology of violent dying—that without a sense of hopeful meaning, or the capacity to calm oneself, or the capacity to control death imagery after a violent dying, the survivor cannot accommodate to the dying event. We owe the basis of our dynamic understanding of the effects of violent dying to these three authors.

The DSM model, which emphasizes a diagnosis rather than a dynamic understanding of the patient, has diminished the significance of most life events, including violent dying. There is no focus for a dynamic understanding of the unique effects or specifics of treatment of violent dying in such an inflexible scheme. Though the DSM disregards the personalized processing of external stressors, it does insist on an objective inventory of measurable responses to stress. The measurement of signs and symptoms encouraged by the DSM protocol has strengthened the validity and reliability in studies of family members after violent dying by objectively documenting their responses of trauma, grief and depression.

Homicide appears to be the most distressing form of violent death for the surviving family member. Suicide is followed by a more isolating and complicated task of explaining the death, and accidental death is more enraging when the deceased was not at fault and there is so little punishment or retribution for the perpetrator.

In recent years there has been a blending of the conceptual focus on family members surviving natural dying to include both trauma and loss as shared dimensions of a common response to death. Though the focus on dying is becoming multidimensional, investigators have not considered the psychological response to violent dying as separate from natural dying. There is abundant anecdotal evidence suggesting that violent dying is associated with higher and more sustained levels of trauma distress, and the task of documenting that difference becomes more comprehensible as investigators accept that responses of loss *and* trauma are dimensions of any death.

Finally, researchers need to include a dynamic formulation in their explanatory model. It is the caring identification with the person who has been killed that underlies non-accommodation. Without a caring connection, a violent death is an item for the news instead of a story that we need to restore ourselves around.

Foretelling Clinical Challenges

Since violent dying involves human intention or neglect and is followed by widespread community effects, why not consider it as preventable death with public causes and consequences? Seen in this wider context, the causes of violent dying extend beyond the individuals directly involved in the killing to include the entire community. Appreciating that violent dying is an event with public health antecedents and consequences allows us to look beyond its immediate spectacle. The spectacle of violent dying, isolated from its origins and effects, is capitalized upon by the news and entertainment industry, or narrowly investigated and punished by our politicians and social agencies. The isolated action or intention of violent dying is a tiny part of its story.

A recent epidemiological study of a large urban community (Breslau, 1998) showed that the sudden, unexpected death of a loved one was a far more important cause of Posttraumatic Stress Disorder than any other event in the community (including criminal assault and rape)—accounting for nearly one third of PTSD cases.

Because there are long-term health effects in family members, and an enormous expenditure of energy and community resources in the investigation, trial, and punishment of violent death, why is there no public health initiative (1) preventing violent dying before it happens (**primary prevention**), (2) identifying community members for early treatment who are at risk for disabling effects following the violent death of a loved one (**secondary prevention**) and (3) providing rehabilitation and education for community members in the aftermath of a violent death (**tertiary prevention**)?

This public health model of prevention provides a framework for managing potential, immediate, and long-term effects of communicable diseases or toxins. As an example, typhoid fever can be prevented by separating drinking wells from septic systems (primary prevention) or, in a typhoid epidemic, families drinking from the same water source can be tested and given antibiotics if infected (secondary prevention) and finally, the community can be educated about the source and effects of the infection to prevent its recurrence (tertiary prevention). Applying this preventive model to the factors responsible for violent death and its effects is telling, not because violent dying is a bacteria or chemical toxin, but because by viewing violent dying as a part of a larger interconnected story, we can better understand why it began and when and how we can intervene.

☐ Primary Prevention: Guns, Cars, Abuse, and Poverty

At least three factors combine in over 50% of violent deaths: substance abuse, firearms, or motor vehicles. Intoxication with drugs and/or alcohol is associated with more than half of motor vehicle deaths and homicides, and firearms cause more than half of all homicides and suicides. Cars, guns, and substance abuse are potent risk factors for violent death, particularly for males between the ages of 15 to 34 where they account for almost all of dying. Despite considerable social pressure and educational resources for preparing our children for the risks of substance abuse, motor vehicle accidents and violence, these factors still combine to create a violent death rate in the U.S. unmatched by any other industrialized country (Department of Health and Human Services, 1997).

The United States continues to follow flawed and contradictory regulations:

1. It is obvious that our national policy of declaring "war on drugs" has been as ineffective in controlling their distribution or use, as the 18th Amendment and its regulation of alcohol. Despite our absolute prohibition of drug distribution, drug availability has soared, and the billions of dollars our country spends on interdiction and the imprisonment of drug traffickers has had very little positive effect in protecting the private citizen or the public.
2. The public outcry regarding the 2nd Amendment infringement of gun owners seems a mirrored reversal—with few exceptions, every adult has a constitutional right to purchase any sort of gun, because the private right to defend yourself from a potential "war" or violent con-

frontation with others takes precedence over the soaring rates of gun deaths and the risk of being killed by unlicensed handguns.

3. Legislation, enforcement, and control of those who drink and drive are caught in a similar dilemma of the 4th Amendment—rights of privacy and autonomy—counterbalanced by public rights of safety and protection. The legal definition of sobriety and the consequences of driving while intoxicated are much less restrictive and punitive in the U.S. than in most other countries.

Perhaps the strident conviction that our private choice takes precedence over our responsibility to others is a reflection of our cultural veneration of independence. Alcohol, drugs, cars, and firearms represent a strong symbol of independence, particularly masculine independence and virility. Many Americans are enraged by any suggestion that access to substances, cars, or firearms might be subject to regulation. Our country was founded on our "right" to resist social oppression, and there is a persistence in the myth that, like the pioneer, we have an obligation to protect ourselves and our family with a gun (now a concealed weapon instead of a trusty revolver) and unregulated access to travel (now a car instead of our faithful horse) and finally to a "good time" (now drugs or mixed drinks instead of a jug of moonshine). Any effort to regulate these icons from our past is viewed as a direct challenge to one's honor or freedom.

Intoxicants, violent weapons, and excessive speed have been risk factors for violent dying for thousands of years and will remain so. They cannot be expunged by any border or enforcement. There will always be a segment of any population, particularly young men, who will insist on combining them. Regulating their use and abuse will remain a constant social challenge. There is no absolute policy or regulation that can assure a primary prevention of violent dying by eradicating the lethal combination of substance abuse, cars, and guns.

There is no question that the media and entertainment industry also contribute, in a less direct way, to the promotion of violent dying. This industry makes enormous profits in presenting violence as a powerful and glorified act that measurably promotes violence. In absolving themselves from any responsibility for this unfortunate promotion, they cite the public's 1st Amendment rights as justification. They maintain that the public has a right to attend to or turn away from whatever is offered; the media are simply responding to what the public wants. It seems that they are correct because our citizens cannot keep themselves from watching. Violent dying and mayhem account for nearly 50% of local news, and television cartoons and dramas continue to highlight violent themes. The media and entertainment industry recognize that the spectacle of violent dying holds a voyeuristic fascination for our culture—and they are simply exercising their entrepreneurial obligation to capitalize on the opportunity.

Generations from now, when the demand for private autonomy might not prevail so strongly over the public good—when we are as concerned for our children as we are for our private entitlements—there might be more balanced social strategies for regulation and intervention. Future strategies will not be based on military and athletic metaphors of "the war on drugs," "just say no," "guns don't kill—people kill," or "three strikes—you're out." Present strategies based on simplistic metaphors are shortsighted and shallow. People who kill others usually have a long history of substance abuse, impulsive and destructive behavior, and childhood histories of abuse and neglect. There is often an extensive history of accumulated personal and social risk factors long ignored as opportunities for primary intervention. In future years we might have proven interventions for high-risk families, where the causes of violence and substance abuse often begin. Until then, we are wasting resources on avoidant and punitive policies that are motivated more by popularity than reason.

There must be more enforcement of regulations. Children, adolescents, and high-risk adults need regulated access to substances, firearms, vehicles, or media violence because their potential violence will have public health effects. Yet this regulation is not forthcoming from the politicians or businesses that benefit directly or indirectly from their profits. Presumably, as with the tobacco industry that aggressively lobbied to prevent regulation, there will be a series of class action lawsuits to force industry regulation or pay the price for the public health consequences of their monetary success.

Approaching violent dying as a public health problem allows the community to intervene with the goal of prevention. By considering behaviors of violence as social derivatives as well as social transgressions, the community can intervene with caring as well as deterrence. That is the way our society considers the violent dying of suicide. If someone attempts suicide in the United States, each state responds with a legal insistence that the attempter be detained and treated. That attempt at violent dying is viewed as an aberrant act associated with a medical disorder that requires confinement and attention—not one, but both. Those who are suicidal need to be isolated and protected from their violent potential until and unless they can be helped to regulate that potential themselves.

This is not to suggest that the social causes of criminal violent dying can be isolated and controlled, or the behaviors of killing can be eradicated, as if violent dying were a disease. In many instances the social and psychological causes of violent dying are too ingrained to be primarily prevented or secondarily treated.

The greatest risk factor for criminal violence beyond the direct effects of drugs and alcohol, guns and cars, is a childhood history of abuse and neglect (Currie, 1998). Our community's capacity to prevent the sacrifice of young children to the social and psychological determinants of violence must begin before they are born and continue during the first five years of their life. Preventive intervention after age five is significantly less effective (Rivara & Farrington, 1995). If our country were truly committed to preventing violence, it would begin by truly caring for abused children.

A comprehensive and long-term preventive social program for child abuse and neglect would take many years, requiring a major social and monetary commitment to a neglected portion of our population—disadvantaged mothers and their small children. Diverting some of the billions of dollars wasted on controlling drugs and warehousing criminals to preventive programs of treatment and social support for young families at high risk for violence and substance abuse is long over-due. Mandating treatment of chemical dependency, rigorous regulation of handguns and assault weapons or impounding the car and revoking the license of anyone with a DWI will probably reduce the potential for violent dying, but those regulations can't directly stop the "soul death" of the young child who is trapped by poverty, abuse and abandonment. A child's sense of purpose and confidence in their future, and respect for their own life or the lives of others, is diminished by persistent abuse and neglect. Until our society considers the nurturance and protection of the vulnerable child as the most fundamental right, taking priority over the 1st, 2nd and 4th Amendment rights of adults, we will continue to waste the lives of these young children until it is too late to prevent their brutal behaviors of intoxication and killing (Gilligan, 1997).

☐ Secondary Prevention: Indentification and Intervention

In previous chapters, we reviewed the psychological effects of violent dying on family members and the prolonged signs and symptoms of non-accommodation. The initial goal of secondary prevention would be to identify community members who have already been exposed to violent dying who would be at greatest risk for developing dysfunctional responses. Clinical reports and empirical studies show that mothers of children who have died violently are at greatest risk for developing high levels of trauma distress that persist for many years, and younger mothers with a developmental history of abuse and neglect and previous psychiatric intervention are at even higher risk. There is also impressive evidence that children of parents who died violently are at similar risk because, like mothers, they share a primary bond of attachment with the deceased (Eth & Pynoos, 1994). It is the strong emotional connection, as givers and receivers of attachment that makes parents and children more vulnerable to its traumatic interruption with violent dying. The intense trauma distress spontaneously subsides in all but a small number of family members who become so dysfunctional that they seek assistance, but mothers and children will probably be most affected.

Once a highly distressed and dysfunctional family member is identified, secondary prevention begins with the reinforcement of resilience followed by a restorative retelling of the living imagery of the deceased to counterbalance the reenactment imagery of his or her dying.

An early systematic screen for comorbid disorders of depression, anxiety, or substance abuse alerts the clinician to the need for specific medications or therapies to manage concurrent clinical disorders. Clinicians would welcome specific biologic testing and targeted medications. Until then, we will continue to use combinations of medications and develop more specific interventions of support, but a major advancement in managing the biologic dysregulation of trauma remains an enormous challenge

A preliminary protocol for secondary prevention outlines a *clinical strategy* that identifies members of the community at high risk (highly attached family members—particularly mothers and children) to assess dysfunctional responses of distress (trauma and separation), or comorbid psychiatric disorders (anxiety, depression, or substance abuse) and offers specific interventions of medication or short-term therapy to restore health. A short-term intervention with group or individual therapy for the family member during the investigation and trial of the violent dying usually precedes intervention for persistent trauma and separation distress. This strategy of secondary prevention is different than the generic response of support and debriefing offered to anyone and everyone connected with the deceased at the site of the violent dying. Instead, there are specific criteria of risk, distress or disorder that are established before offering focused, short-term interventions.

Another challenge for the systematic secondary prevention of the effects of violent dying on members of the community is the organization of a *centralized clinical service*. Every major urban center has a sufficient number of violent deaths to justify such a service. Without a centralized service, the individual clinician discovers that it is very difficult to offer comprehensive care. Clinicians need ongoing contact with numerous agencies and parties that are also involved in the violent dying, and assistance with specialized restorative techniques. A centralized service can develop a more efficient system for assessment, referral and restoration with experienced primary and consulting clinicians. The organization of a community service also provides a forum for referral and flow of information between community agencies (police, prosecuting attorneys, victims' assistance services, medical examiner's office, therapists, support groups), so that secondary prevention can be better coordinated.

Within a community-based service, members of the community who are at high risk can be followed for ongoing attention. It is not unusual for family members to have delayed responses of distress. They were so preoccupied with the pragmatic issues of caring for other family members or the investigation and trial of the perpetrator in the first year or two after the death, that the secondary prevention they refused the year before would now be welcomed. It is not realistic or necessary, to follow those who refuse assessment for more than a year or two, but those who need delayed attention are grateful for a service that continues to offer help rather than abandoning them. Family members are familiar enough with abandonment by the media, police, courts, and friends after the spectacle of the trial has finished, so it is comforting to know that ongoing care is available.

☐ Tertiary Prevention: Support Groups, Victims' Compensation, and Rehabilitating the Perpetrator

Tertiary prevention occurs after the crisis related to the violent dying has subsided. The community members who need longer-term assistance can be rehabilitated and the community can examine their survival and learn how to prevent the crisis from recurring.

Until the 1970s, there were no social agencies or institutions in the United States to serve the function of longer-term support, education and empowerment after violent dying until the *mutual support group* movement began. Groups of family members joined by a common tragedy, with a collective commitment to surviving the aftermath of violent dying, offered a setting of empathic caring where each member shared how the dying had changed them.

Mutual support groups were the first to serve as ombudsmen for the confused family—a function now called "victims' services" and later mandated by most criminal-judicial agencies. They also served as potent social advocates by collectively pressuring their legislatures to tighten laws that would prevent violent dying, to enact harsher sentences, and to enable the family members to have a more active role during the investigation, trial and sentencing of the perpetrator.

The effectiveness of the mutual support group movement came from the direct and unqualified promise of helping. There has been no profit motive because members implicitly recognized that they needed to help and be helped by others who had experienced a similar dying instead of consulting with a professional. They needed to deal with the effects of the violent dying—not some problem from their childhood, or their marriage, or any of the "issues" that psychotherapists are trained to treat. Indeed, it was partially because of the irrelevancy of psychotherapy that family members spontaneously met in a group forum where other members had an immediate and intuitive understanding of their tragedy.

There is no question that mutual support groups have provided a valuable service of tertiary prevention for bereaved family members (Marmar, 1988), but it is unfortunate that they have been isolated from the support of surrounding clinical and service agencies. Perhaps a centralized clinical service could encourage more cross referral of difficult cases, and training in short-term, restorative strategies applied within groups meeting for spontaneous and mutual support. Offering a centralized service for violent dying, where family members could be referred for screening and consideration of medication, would also be a useful resource for support groups as an additional service, not a replacement, for their participation in the mutual support program.

Establishing a more cooperative working relationship between mutual support groups and resources of clinical and community support is a challenge filled with preventive and educational potential. However, this rapprochement cannot begin until clinicians offer short-term, relevant strategies for screening and intervention that are clearly and concisely related to violent death. These strategies need to be effective and simple enough that non-clinicians can apply them, and the indications and opportunity for clinical support need to be defined, available, and without charge.

In 1984, because of the strong lobbying efforts of support groups and associated organizations representing victims of physical and sexual abuse, our national congress approved funding for the Department of Justice to establish the *Office for Victims of Crime*. This office is mandated to provide financial retribution and service for adults and children. Funds are drawn from the financial penalties collected from federal felons, not from taxes. This money (approximately $250 million per year) is divided and distributed between all 50 states (each state administers the money through an agency of their choice) for burial expenses, financial support for destitute families, and payment for requisite medical and mental health services for disorders related to the crime. While most of these funds are designated and spent in serving women and children who have been physically and sexually abused, those who are left to accommodate to a criminal death are eligible as well. Unfortunately, only the immediate family members of innocent victims of criminal dying are covered by victims' compensation. This arbitrary decision dismisses the emotional aftermath in the immediate family of someone killed while committing a crime, and that family may be as overwhelmed and innocent as the family of the victim.

There is a marked discrepancy in the range of benefits and requirements for coverage between states. Without specific guidelines for assessment and support, each state agency arbitrarily creates its own. For example, the number of approved treatment sessions for a family member after a criminal death is limited to six in the State of Connecticut, while the State of Washington approves at least thirty before insisting on a more rigorous review. Washington State recently increased the number of treatment sessions from twelve to thirty, after appointing a committee of clinicians and victims' compensation officials from across the state to establish treatment guidelines specific for crime victims. After thoroughly reviewing the treatment literature on treating crime victims and the pattern of charges for victims' compensation in Washington State, the committee was able to recommend a range of benefits and treatment strategies based upon objective clinical and financial information. These guidelines were approved by the legislature and sent to every licensed mental health agency and practitioner in an updated and referenced manual and clinical review.

There are definite advantages to developing localized guidelines for each area, because each state has different patterns of criminal activity and specific clinical needs and resources. Also, the very process of developing guidelines and benefits, as a locally convened group, ensures the active involvement of the surrounding clinicians, as partners in developing the guidelines rather than the passive followers of external regulation. Perhaps the Department of Justice should insist that each state periodically convene such a committee as a quality control assurance that clinicians who have ready access to solid clinical strategies are appropriately supporting crime victims. That would be preferable to the development of generic guidelines and their enforcement.

Finally, the members of the community who are completely abandoned and isolated from any preventive intervention are those who have committed a violent death. Despite the harsh sentences and possibility of legal execution for murder in the U.S. (27% of murderers serve life sentences without parole or are on death row; Currie, 1998, p. 45), the majority will be released. Unlike a disease or a toxin that can be exterminated or disposed, someone paroled for committing a violent death still lives and will live with us again. Not surprisingly, in this "get tough on crime" era of mandated sentencing and punishment, there is no systematic program within high-security prisons to rehabilitate murderers before their release, beyond estimating their potential for murdering again. Why doesn't our society have an obligation to help people understand and regulate their murderous impulses before releasing them back into the community? The community needs to be reassured that a murderer's release is contingent upon some basic effort at rehabilitation. Whoever is to be released after committing a violent death should, at the very least, have a commitment to achieving long-term sobriety, learning to read, to mastering a vocational skill, to controlling their anger, to helping providing restitution for their victim's family—the elements of a positive contract between the inmate and the community before release with clear conditions and consequences for its continuance or termination and return to prison. Our courts and prisons need to provide requisite rehabilitation, communication with the family of the deceased, and probation planning for reintegrating the offender back into the community before release. While execution or life imprisonment is equivalent to primary prevention (eradication or isolation of the cause of violent dying), rehabilitating those imprisoned is an extension of primary prevention—like attenuating the lethality of a pathogen or toxin before releasing it back into the community.

Those who kill will return to us, and the time that they serve in prison should prepare them to be not only safe, but productive members of society. Often they return to their role as parent, and rehabilitation might stop them from perpetrating the same neglect and abuse with their children that they had suffered themselves.

☐ Community-Based Service, Training, and Restoration for Clinicians

Violent dying from homicide, suicide, or accident is sufficiently frequent and specific in its effects on family members to justify a specialized community resource for immediate, intermediate and rehabilitative assistance. Violent dying from any cause (homicide, suicide, or accident) can be supported with a common strategy of secondary prevention. A centralized community service could offer the same strategy of screening and intervention for any sort of violent death, and coordinate the relevant social and clinical agencies in offering a spectrum of services—for a family after the violent death of one of its members—or a community of survivors and families after a widespread violent death like a school shooting or a terrorist bombing or an airplane crash. A specialized, community resource would need monetary support so that it could coordinate free services to members of the community, since a disproportionate number of those devastated by violent dying cannot afford mental health services.

There have been several community disasters with massive casualties where a comprehensive support service has been summoned. The bombing of the Federal Office Building in Oklahoma City in 1995 and the Columbine School shooting in Denver in 1999 brought vigorous community responses of support, and while funding and consultations from external agencies supported these services, the primary initiative and structure of support was local. Presumably these support services could be more efficiently implemented if there were an existent support program for violent dying that played a clinical role in organizing secondary and tertiary prevention. Such a service could remain in place indefinitely to respond to the ongoing needs of families.

The purposes of such a centralized service would include the recruitment, training, and support of service providers. While full-time personnel would be limited to a small administrative staff and several clinicians in order to provide assessment, consultation and specialty groups, there would be an overarching network of referral with clinicians in the community available for intermediate care and longer-term rehabilitation.

A centralized service would also offer periodic workshops, lectures, and ongoing case consultation to the clinical community. These sorts of training opportunities would not only reinforce clinical competence, but also serve as a wellspring of professional resilience. Local clinical case conferences would bring a return of therapeutic perspective for the clinician isolated and immersed in the repetitive reenactment experience of family members. Excessive immersion in reenactment retelling diminishes resilience in both the teller and the listener. Clinicians need to regain their own accommodation, and develop skills to avoid losing their equanimity and boundaries when they return to their practices.

Many clinicians are very unpracticed at caring for themselves. They are startled to hear that they need to ask themselves the same questions they ask their patients:

"Should you work over the lunch hour? Don't you need to get away?"

"What do you do to give your mind a rest from all this trauma?"

"How do you say no to a new patient when your plate is too full of trauma?"

"How can you help someone else with his or her story when you can't stand to hear it?"

"Who takes care of you?"

Clinician burn-out is hardly surprising because many clinicians have such strong caregiving tendencies that they fail to tend to their own needs. Supporting stressed clinicians is another task of tertiary prevention. Clinicians need to be restored from their vicarious trauma before they return to their caregiving role in the community. While the rehabilitation of murderers is ignored because of their criminality, the "rehabilitation" of traumatized clinicians is ignored because of their altruism. In either case, an unwarranted stereotype exaggerates the avoidance of their needs.

In this era of professional veneration of the specialist, it is difficult to resist the idea of standardized training and testing to become a "certified" violent death or traumatic death specialist. However, it seems wiser to delay specialization until and unless there is a firmer database to validate its special effects and strategies of treatment. At this point, our clinical experience and theory are too preliminary to justify categorical statements. It is better to remain open to novel insights and approaches. Specialization risks narrowing the ranks and thinking of clinicians and investigators.

☐ A Summary Illustration: The Cocoanut Grove Disaster Revisited

Rather than dryly recounting the professional challenges of violent dying let's reconsider how they might be enacted in a community disaster we have already described. What if the Cocoanut Grove fire, with its tragedy of 491 deaths, repeated itself? What would we do differently if we could create a comprehensive service for those survivors affected by the death of loved ones?

Even today, the sudden death of that many people by that same event would be overwhelming to the services of any major, metropolitan area. The same mayhem of sirens and speeding vehicles of every kind would descend on trauma centers and emergency rooms. The same process of desperate triage and rows of dead bodies would unfold. Certainly more would survive with advanced life support and treatment in specialized burn and intensive care units, but just as many would die from acute, pulmonary thermal injuries.

As it stands today, each hospital would offer psychiatric services, and the large trauma centers might have a psychiatric staff prepared to manage the acute psychological needs of the survivors. Survivors would have an opportunity for psychiatric assessment, but not many would be evaluated unless they requested referral or were obviously disturbed. It is very doubtful that each survivor would be interviewed before his or her release, unless there was a local clinical investigator—a contemporary version of Drs. Adler or Lindemann—prepared and funded to launch a prospective study. Most survivors would be released, and forgotten.

There would be more community focus on replaying the spectacle than in 1942. For several weeks after the disaster the media would be obsessed with televised images of the smoking ruins of the nightclub and interviews with survivors as they repeated their reenactment stories. The national media would include hour-long specials to describe details of how the tragedy happened and how it could have been avoided, including the predictable interviews with grief experts who would quote the stages of grief and preach the importance of crying and expressing sadness and anger. Attorneys would gather around the survivors of the fire and family members of the deceased, impressing them with the opportunities of recovering financial compensation from the owners of the nightclub who recklessly disregarded safety regulations.

A community-based, clinical service of support after violent dying would respond to more than the spectacle of the fire and those who escaped. To be sure, each hospitalized survivor would be offered an assessment and screening, but when 491 people die in a horrific fire, not only hospitalized survivors need emotional support; primary and extended family members are left to retell the story of those last moments of their loved ones—as they burned and suffocated. Hundreds of family members would be left to reconstruct the nightmarish drama of someone they loved and protected—dying while trapped, smothered, and seared.

With the cooperation of the medical examiner's office, a centralized clinical service could contact every survivor and every family of the 491 fatalities to offer ongoing support, consultation, or intervention. Each family would be sent a brief letter of condolence followed by a phone call and an offer of assistance and support at no charge. The media could announce the availability of the supportive service, and members of the staff would be available for media interviews to clarify the common response of reenactment imagery and the importance of restorative retelling. Hopefully, the television coverage of the tragedy would avoid repeated replaying of death-related imagery, knowing how traumatizing this was for many family members (Cote & Simpson, 2000).

The number of direct survivors and grieving family members might total more than 2,000 individuals. However, only a small minority, perhaps 15–20% (300 or 400 individuals) would request assistance. Knowing that mothers and children would be at greatest risk for developing dysfunctional response would make them a targeted subgroup for support. Others, with a delayed response of trauma and separation, would likely request help during the second or third year after the fire. The centralized office would provide initial assessment, including screening and specialized group interventions. Through existent working relationships with community agencies and surrounding clinicians, coordinated support could be arranged for each high-risk survivor.

☐ Restorative Retelling of the Survivors

Finally, we would not forget the reenactment stories of that horrible night of massive dying and how they would be retold in a treatment that included restorative retelling. How would we manage the terrible memory that survivors carried within them? From the case reports of Dr. Adler and Dr. Lindemann (Chapter 8, pp. 107–109), we know the stories retold by two young men who watched their wives perish in the fire. Reviewing how their reenactment stories were either virtually ignored by Dr. Adler, or over-exposed by Dr. Lindemann, highlights the more personalized and adaptive strategy of restorative retelling.

Dr. Adler did not treat the 20-year-old man whose pregnant wife died in the fire, despite noting his mixed response of depression and severe trauma distress with vivid reenactment flashbacks, nightmares, and avoidant behaviors in follow-up visits. Apparently, the young man could not control the reenactment images of his wife's dying and could not tolerate any situation (movie theatres or sirens) that reminded him of the fire. He was clearly impaired—unable to function effectively at work and declared unfit to serve in the military by his draft board—and needed active intervention. His treatment would now include a more rigorous screening for comorbid psychiatric disorders. From his clinical description and persistence of his dysfunction, he probably met criteria for chronic posttraumatic stress disorder and major depression, both of which would respond to medication combined with a targeted therapy to restore his resilience and reduce his distress through gradual exposure and retelling of his traumatic memory of the fire. With his permission, the family of his dead wife would be contacted as well, to not only enlist their support in his restoration, but to offer them help in their adjustment to her death as well.

Dr. Lindemann first saw the 32-year-old man three months after his discharge from the hospital. From his brief description, we can be quite certain that this young man was experiencing severe, delusional guilt about his inability to rescue his wife. It sounds as if he was preoccupied with a fixed and false belief—not only was he primarily responsible for her dying, but his future was "doomed" and he felt he should die to atone for his failure. Delusional guilt and a sense of utter hopelessness are particularly potent risk factors for suicide, and it was appropriate to hospitalize him. However, someone with a psychotic depression, a serious comorbid psychiatric disorder, is not a good candidate for a short-term psychotherapy that encourages the expression of feelings, and particularly not anger. In the midst of a psychosis one cannot accurately define or process overwhelming feelings. Instead of a therapy that encouraged an immersion in the reenactment story of his wife's dying and his impotent rage at himself for failing to rescue her, a therapy involving restorative retelling would actively avoid such a retelling until he was more resilient. Restorative retelling would follow projective psychological testing to document his psychosis, and would initially focus on providing intense support and reassurance.

Biologic treatment of a psychotic depression would now be a priority and would include a major tranquilizer combined with an antidepressant medication. If his delusional guilt and hopelessness worsened over the next two to three weeks, despite adequate medication, and he became increasingly suicidal and unable to eat, drink, or sleep, then electroconvulsive treatment might be considered. While that may sound like an extreme intervention to some readers, an acute, psychotic depression is a potentially fatal disorder—as was sadly the case with this young man. Electroconvulsive treatment remains the most effective and immediate form of treatment for psychotic depression, and he probably would have responded. This is not to deny the dynamic importance of his memory of his wife's dying, and while restorative retelling would be crucial, it would be delayed until his psychosis had cleared.

This strategy, of aggressively treating the young man's psychosis and stabilizing his mind from the chaotic replay of his reenactment story of failing to rescue his wife, probably would have prevented his suicide and another violent death for his family. Not only did they lose their daughter-in-law in the fire, but their son by his own hand. How did Dr. Lindemann offer to support that mother and father when he called to announce that their son had killed himself? That must have been a painful moment, for Dr. Linedemann as well as the family.

I have often wondered what happened to the family members of these two young men and their wives who died. With their own resiliency, and the cohesiveness of their family and community and church, most were probably able to restore themselves. I would predict that the parents, and particularly the mothers of the young women who died in the fire, would have persistent trauma distress each time they recalled how their child died—in total darkness, crushed and burning and smothering. How could they reenact that dying without blaming themselves? Each of them would wonder how they should have kept their child from going there that night. Who listened as their agonizing retelling went on for months or years and guided them in a restorative direction—away from the darkness and the heat and the smothering? Perhaps they were unable to reengage with life with a sense of meaning or purpose because of their absorption in the endless senselessness of that fire. How many suffering family members could we have reached and restored?

☐ The Incongruity of Closure

The beginning of this book promised clarifications rather than a conclusion, and in our brief telling of violent dying there have been several:

1. **The necessity of resilience** for restorative retelling, and the **identification of obstacles** (avoidance, possession and comorbidity) once retelling begins.
2. **Preliminary concepts** to clarify our understanding of the specific effects of violent dying (the paradox of the dying narrative, the mandatory 3 V's - violence, violation & volition -, the multidimensional distresses of trauma and separation, and the neuro-biology of traumatic memory)
3. **Preliminary guidelines** for therapeutic retelling (screening for resilience and risk, reinforcement of resilience through the 3 P's—pacification, partition, and perspective, restorative group and individual interventions, and indications for medication for comorbid disorders).
4. We have joined in the **restorative retelling** of several family members to experience the unique narrative transformation of each person.
5. **Specialized interventions** (short-term group and individual retelling) were described and evidence was presented of their effectiveness for adults and children.

We also considered how these guiding clinical clarifications began, through a focused review of the literature of early investigators. Finally, we've allowed ourselves to imagine how these clarifications might be altered and applied in the future within an entire community.

While each of these clarifications may shed some light on, or briefly penetrate, the shroud of ambiguity wrapped around the suffering of someone after violent dying, we cannot pretend a final answer or resolution. A strong and implicit theme within this book has been to better prepare the reader—as clinician, family member, or general reader—to accept that we can help, but not cure.

Retelling my wife's suicide, or my attempts to restore the retelling of my patients—and even the stories of survivors of the Cocoanut Grove fire that I've never met—is the beginning of a dynamic, unending reconstruction. Retelling violent dying never stops. Retelling forces the teller into a role within a surreal drama that can be revised, but not finished. Within a violent dying story, even death brings no closure. Death may disintegrate the life of the person, but it cannot stop the retelling of that person's dying—those last moments of his or her living. Each time I retell my own violent dying story of Julie, or join in the retelling of Valerie, Charles, Robert, Pat, Ralph, Maggie, or the survivors of the Cocoanut Grove fire, the imaginary story of what the loved one experienced during the last moments of life cannot be closed. His or her dying persists, as an imaginary and untenable story retold by those of us who cannot accept that someone we protectively loved died without and despite us—alone and helpless. It is the solitary drama of our loved ones' dying, disconnected from the story of our caring presence while they were dying, that cannot be reconciled, no matter how many times we retell.

Recognizing that the ordeal of retelling the violent dying of a loved one is a paradox reorients us. If we can't change the substance of the story, we need to change ourselves within the retelling. This begins with the right of ownership—this story of violent dying belongs to us, and somehow we have to find a voice and a place for ourselves. We need enough resilience to reestablish safety, and a time and space to exist within the imaginary reenactment of the violent dying story before starting. Once we exist in the retelling, we have an opportunity to realign ourselves with what happens within the drama. We cannot make it "unhappen," but we can imagine ourselves rescuing, retaliating, comforting, scolding, holding, soothing, reassuring—and finally, relinquishing—rather than saying goodbye.

We were closer to this sort of generative, imaginary self-revision in the retelling of stories when we were children, but the rudiments of magical and imaginary retelling remain. All of us, children and adults, can stabilize our self image from the corrosive possession stories of reenactment, remorse, retaliation, or protection through an imaginary retelling that reconnects us with our role as living and vital.

Imaginative and restorative retelling does not lead towards a closing, but rather an opening—away from the chaos of dying; toward the coherence of living. It may be an opening for the expression of repressed rage or sadness, but it aims beyond our momentary feelings to connect with sources of living engagement around and within us. Rather than closure, restoration aims at opening and confirming that we are alive. That reconnection transforms us as active participants in our own life story, with a return of hope and purpose.

Though we author and enact our own life story, it is changed by the story of violent dying—like a subliminal theme or tone that cannot be seamlessly joined within the narrative of our living. The story of violent dying, like an unwelcome stowaway, remains alive within us. It stirs a dissonance. No matter how much of my remembrance of Julie is connected with the time and space of living, there is no closing my connection with her dying. Her dying memory no longer floods my awareness while awake or asleep, but there are dark moments when it is rekindled, like a twisted shadow of her living—miscast and jagged. And traces of my possessions of remorse and protectiveness lurk in that shadow as well. I still can't forgive myself for not saving her (there *must* have been something I could have done), and I will always overprotect my babies (I *must* keep them safe, no matter that they are now adults and safe by themselves).

☐ The Artifact of Words

Rather than closing this book with too many words, I want to summon transforming metaphors of opening and reconnection. Words cleave experience into discrete bits, and too many words cleave too deeply, dividing what is discrete about a human experience into something categorical. When we first retell a violent dying, our ability to name what happened creates an experiential separation from what we cannot tolerate. That is an artifact of naming or analyzing experience—creating a separable difference. But in a restorative retelling, as we are in the process of transforming ourselves, we need generative metaphors or synthesizing images beyond the words, to return our sense of integrity.

Objectifying words diminish the power of what is subjectively joined. Even when words aim at unifying experience, they distort it (Bohm, 1996). Poets and playwrights, determined to create an imaginary image or drama, try to reconnect us with an underlying unification beyond their words. So do therapists. A great poem, a powerful play, or an effective session of therapy share in this transformation of awareness (Spence, 1982). Words of poets and playwrights and therapists may recount scenes of dying and death, but in their retelling they include images that transform the reader, the audience, or the patient (Hillman, 1983). Artful retelling of violent dying shifts the telling perspective from witness to participant and, finally, to a survivor changed by the retelling. Artless poetry or drama and ineffective therapy fail to include imaginative and transforming imagery beyond the spectacle of dying and death.

In our contemporary culture, written words and numbers form the basis of our system for communicating. The instrumentation of words through media sound-bites or computers allows an extension and speed of communication, but robs us of the unifying presence of the other person as we converse. The technology of communication may be wondrously efficient at one level, but alienating of others. Too many words divide us from each other and from our own totality. This informational disconnect from multiple and simultaneous levels of experience came with the written word. Without written words there was a more inherent unification of experience. With an oral understanding of the world, the secular, the sacred, and the spiritual were one piece.

I imagine that if I had been a member of a preliterate culture my experience of Julie's violent dying would have been very different. I wonder how I would have adjusted to her suicide if we had lived on Bainbridge Island before the written word?

Our island would not have been named after a British naval surveyor, but for parts of its shore that were covered by "white rocks" or "salmon berries." Naming would be functionally integrated with some visible feature or repeated activity. We would be members of a coastal tribe whose ancestors we venerated—a mystical, divine tribe that ruled the earth and sky and ocean now and forever, and timelessly watched over us. Our connection to our extended family and tribe would be clear and deep, like the water before our cedar longhouse. Our culture would value the welfare of the clan above the success of the individual, committing us to care for one another before caring for ourselves. We would be dependent on one another and on nature to provide the food we gathered and caught, and we would give sacrifices to the divine spirits to ensure their continued provision before we ate.

Since there were no written words, major events like births, deaths, or contracts between families and clans would be mutually celebrated through ceremonies, called potlatches, which involved speeches of mutual respect and the sharing of gifts. The family hosting the celebration would provide gifts and food as a sign of the family's distributive power. Part of the ceremony would include dances and ritualized performances of myths. The host would appear in ceremonial dress and mask of a spiritual intermediary (a raven, a whale, an eagle, a bear). Through the mask and the dance, the audience and the dancer would transform themselves within the power of the invoked spirit.

Because there were no written records, we cannot know precisely how death or violent dying would have affected Julie or me. Deaths must have been very common from infections (particularly after childbirth and during infancy), accidental drowning, and frequent warfare. Presumably a gathering of our family and clan to begin a ritual of mourning would have immediately surrounded us. Whatever the cause of dying, natural or unnatural, our family would be involved from start to finish and would have an active role in retelling the violent dying story.

Suicide must have occurred, as it always has in every society. Perhaps living was so demanding and the dying of an infant so common, that our baby's death might have been less overwhelming for Julie. Or when she could not survive her own despair and killed herself, there would be a spiritual explanation—that she had taken her own life to reclaim her lost spirit that was somewhere near our baby. There would have been a large gathering and an extensive ceremony where we danced and communicated with her lost spirit.

For days or weeks, I would have had reenactment fantasies and dreams of her dying. If I could no longer sleep or carry out my duties, my family and I might decide that we needed to consult with a shaman, a practitioner who specialized in reconnecting tribal members with spirits. I assume that the shaman would diagnose Julie's spirit as damaged because of her unnatural death. Oral history is filled with references to the unhappy ghosts of those who died violently—their spirit unable to rest until the trauma of their dying had been repaired. Shamans carved their own masks (often of the octopus, the kingfisher, or the river otter—animals that communicated with dead spirits in the underworld) and occasionally masks of the deceased that communicated directly with their troubled spirit. Wearing the mask of her face and dancing over me with sacred objects, the shaman and I would restore Julie's lost spirit, so that she would stop robbing me of my own. Through the shaman, and the power of the mask ceremony, I would merge in an imaginary reunion with her absent-presence, to reassure her that I wanted her to be strong and well again.

Of course, this sort of ritualized dance and restoration of angry spirits continues to this day in many parts of the world, including highly Westernized and literate countries. After the violent dying of a family member, we need transforming imagery and healing rituals. If our contemporary culture cannot provide it because of its lack of connection with a sustaining sacred or spiritual tradition, then family members who cannot accommodate to their persistent death imagery will seek it from alternative sources. Very few of us believe in ghosts or spirits, but all of us know that a most effective way of restoring ourselves from violent dying begins by confronting our own ghost story—the private retelling of the dying. The shaman and his mask and our healing ritual would allow me to connect with my private projection of Julie's dying image, and his reassurance that we could retell this story and restore ourselves in the process would strengthen my autonomy from what had happened.

There would be nothing supernatural about such a process. I don't believe that our ceremony would change Julie's spirit or her dying, but our mutual participation in retelling would allow me to change and realign myself to my possession memory of her dying, and reconnect me with my own vitality.

The Unifying Image of Water

Every culture contains powerful, preverbal symbols that draw multiple levels of experience into a singular coherence. They may refer to an image of nature (recurring celestial movements, dynamic seasonal changes, tidal ebb and flows), or nurture (love and affiliation within a family, clan, or country), or spirit (timeless reincarnation or permanent vitality beyond death).

Nature is my favorite unifying image, and water has been the most comforting and stabilizing for me. This is not so much from its physicality (its taste, its smell, its noise, or its touch), or from its essential functions (to drink, to wash, to dissolve, or to soak). It is in my contemplation of floating on its surface that I feel most connected with nature and my total self.

My connection is even stronger if the surface is pulled and foamed. There is nothing that sweeps my mind more quickly of words, than swirling on the racing surface of a river in a kayak, particularly when the river narrows into a descending rapid that drives me forward and down. Once I have committed myself to its power and current, my mind and body join in an absolute and cooperative concentration—to keep me within its boundary and on its surface—and away from the dark rocks. There is no time for thought until I nose into its flatness at the end of the rapid. Now my hands shake as I feel the elation of releasing myself from its grip.

For most of us, that moment of choosing to merge with a strong natural force rather than avoiding or resisting, is all too rare. Our culture prepares us for a resistance against nature and natural forces like grief, more than a wordless joining and sustaining of our self within it.

Throughout this book I have made reference to the reinforcement of resilience through the experience of joining and connection as a first step in mastery. For me, the transforming reconnection with water is my wordless joining and there is something ineffably transcendent in that experience. Others may experience transcendence in their sense of prevailing stability by connecting with a sacred or spiritual belief, but nature also brings a direct and sensible experience. Nature connects me with an open and naked perceptiveness in contrast to the consciousness required by belief. I never know what nature will show me. My momentary experience of nature is filled with wordless novelty.

Relearning the importance of floating and flowing was an epiphany for me when I was learning how to body surf. By remaining calm and floating on my back, I could stay on the surface until the tidal surge spent itself, and only then could I begin to swim for shore. The preverbal image of floating and flowing on the surface of a powerful current is helpful to anyone swept helplessly in their own reenactment imagery. Recognizing that there is a safe place in this overwhelming story—at first on its surface, not in its depths where one cannot sustain oneself—brings a sense of transcendence and self-control.

The unifying image of water as a transforming connection is different from the sacred or spiritual unifying image of an afterlife. The image of life after death not only releases the victim and the teller from the dying story, but also reinforces the avoidance of retelling. There is an inherent economy and simplicity in the image of an afterlife. After all, if the deceased is released from the story, there is less need to retell it. Why reconstruct and restore the story of the violent dying when the deceased is somewhere safe? Despite the parsimony of this sacred or spiritual transformation, many family members are unable to feel transformed in their sacred or spiritual retelling. Though their loved one is transformed and released from the violent dying story, they remain possessed and cannot forgive themselves or cannot keep themselves from needing to retaliate or protect.

Restorative retelling, based on the unifying image of floating and flowing on the surface of the violent dying story, maintains an indirect connection. It suggests a restorative boundary between the teller and the story. Floating and flowing allows the teller a continuing presence within the violent dying story, and the opportunity for his or her own transformation through retelling. That transforming story is always filled with novelty because it is so personal. Unlike the highly formalized retelling of a sacred or spiritual story that follows a ritualized and transforming plot far removed from the story of the violent dying, restorative retelling deals directly with the role of the teller within the dying plot. Ritual imposes an external order and is incurious; restorative retelling creates an inner reordering and is novel.

Restorative retelling, based on the unifying image of water, includes the clinician as helmsman, navigator, and anchor. In this extended image of unity, the clinician is aware of surrounding referents and is responsible for guiding the retelling towards a safe harbor. Sharing the progress of retelling as if it were a small boat far from shore, the clinician knows how to flow with the available forces of wind and current, and to skirt the shallow shoals and rocks while heading toward landfall. But each restorative retelling follows a unique course. When the teller becomes lost or overwhelmed, the clinician can guide, but not determine, the final course. This is very different from the usual role of the physician, the shaman, the clergy, or the spiritualist who assumes authority and primary responsibility for the entire enterprise. In restorative retelling there is a fundamental premise, that whatever unfolds is under the primary control of the teller—or the story won't be transforming for him or her.

EPILOGUE
While I Am Rowing

As I have become older my restorative connection with water has mellowed. I no longer charge into the ocean to body surf or paddle through rapids. Seniors seek calmer water.

I still live on the same island, and each morning, as the sun first rises, I launch myself from my dock in a rowing scull. While rowing, I am so absorbed in coordinating my movements and balance that I am aware of little beyond the sensation of gliding and the noise of the blades as they enter and release from the ocean. I stay close to shore and wear a life vest in case I capsize, but that is my only concession to the depth of the water. I am so intent on gliding that I rarely think of what suspends me.

It is when I stop to rest that I become more observant and reflective. One morning it occurred to me that sculling on the ocean was a unifying image for my identity. Like the solitary rower, my identity is a dynamic balancing on the surface of something so vast and continuous that it cannot be finally determined. Composed of deep and chaotic forces, my mind can only be aware of the surface phenomena of who "I" am—and the deep and mysterious forces of nature in which it is balanced. My connection with these forces is limited by the boundaries of my senses. I am indirectly aware of their momentary strength and direction, but cannot ultimately know when and where they will swirl me. I cannot know the future. Like the rower who faces where he has been, my mind cannot comprehend time as continuous, but only of the moment or its past.

Julie's suicide was like an enormous, dark wave—deep and chaotic—that swept and overwhelmed me. Momentarily I was thrown from my boat and from my identity. Restoring myself started with my having confidence that I was going to be safe and my determination to get back into the boat. Remaining in the waves would bring exhaustion and despair. On the surface, after baling out my boat, I could row and find my own way back to shore.

145

To some it might seem ironic that the image of water and rowing would be unifying to me in the time and space of Julie's dying. How could her decision to die by surrendering herself to water be transformed by my image of sustaining myself on its surface? Water does not separate me from dying or death—Julie's or my own. I remain suspended from, but connected with, dying in my own depths. Water unifies my experience of my living with dying, and my awareness of that inevitability is calming. Connected with my potential dying and death, I am more open and sensitive to living and life, and I continue to row every morning that the tide and the weather let me.

Every voyage is different. This morning I saw two eagles.

APPENDIX

☐ Violent Dying Support: Screening and Interventions

Helping a highly distressed person after the violent death of a loved one requires a combination of personal support and clinical structure. Reassurance and clear clarification of coping are the primary objectives of early sessions, and clinical assessment cannot begin until the person feels a return of safety and emotional distance from the violent dying. Only then can the person begin to consider evaluating and changing their response to what has happened.

Violent dying support begins with personalized support and guidance, but includes a restorative clinical model and structure. The model focuses on the direct effects of violent dying on distress and offers time limited group interventions. However, before intervention, it is imperative to re-establish a capacity for self-calming and integrity and then to screen for comorbid disorders that might require separate treatment.

Assessment and Screening

We have developed a clinical screening battery to guide the clinician and the client in developing a treatment plan. Specifically, the following five instruments are useful: (1) the Beck Depression Inventory (BDI); (2) the Inventory of Traumatic Grief (ITG); (3) the Death Imagery Scale (DIS); (4) the Impact of Events Scale-Revised (IES-R); and (5) the Drug/Alcohol Screening Test (DAST). These measures were selected because they address the effects of violent dying on bereavement and are simple, self-report measures widely used by other clinicians and researchers in the field.

Scoring and Clinical Implications

1. The BDI is a 21-item instrument that reliably measures clinical depression. A score 0-9 is within normal range. Any score >18 indicates psychiatric consultation and consideration of psychotropic medication.
2. The ITG addresses the synergism between traumatic distress and separation distress. It is our experience that separation distress does not resolve without first moderating traumatic distress. The ITG identifies 19 core symptoms which comprise the range of thoughts and emotions definitive of traumatic grief. A finding of traumatic grief indicates that Restorative Retelling, Criminal Death Support group, or individual support/treatment may be beneficial.
3. Developed by the primary author, the DIS indicates the degree to which individuals experience imagery of reenactment, reunion, rescue and revenge related to police and media reports, further embellished by the individual's projective fantasies. While imagery of reunion, rescue and revenge are common (occurring on a daily or weekly basis in 40% of all survivors within the first six months of the dying) reenactment imagery is significantly more intense and frequent in those who seek treatment (occurring on a daily or weekly basis in 80%). If individuals report reenactment imagery on a daily or a weekly basis, we recommend the Restorative Retelling group or individual support.
4. The IES-R measures the degree and frequency of traumatic distress. The instrument is made up of three subscales: Intrusion, Avoidance, and Hyperarousal that, taken separately and together, suggest possible PTSD, a syndrome not uncommon following the violent dying of a loved one.
5. The DAST is a useful tool that should be interpreted in context. A score >3 warrants discussion with the individual. A current problem of substance abuse must be addressed before the individual participates in Restorative Retelling or Criminal Death Support groups.

The Screening Process

We use the screening battery as an interactive experience, not as a test. Someone with average reading abilities can complete it in about 45 minutes.

Following completion of a group or individual intervention, we meet with each subject to repeat the testing, review the comparative scores, and assess the need for further support.

☐ Interventions

Support after violent dying may include two separate support groups: the first (**Criminal Death Support Group** or **CDS**) for friends and family members who need information and advocacy during the investigation and trial of a violent death, and a second (**Restorative Retelling Group** or **RR**) for friends and family members who need to retell and reprocess their distressing narrative of the dying. Both groups are closed and contain a maximum of ten members who meet for ten, weekly, two-hour sessions. The CDS group is largely composed of members adjusting to the criminal-judicial aftermath of homicide, while the RR group may contain a mixture of members adjusting to the traumatic narrative of any type of violent dying—homicide, suicide or accident.

Criminal Death Support Group

Purpose: For family members and friends who have lost someone in a violent death AND are involved with the criminal justice system. Crime related death differs from any other because of the intense social scrutiny and demand for investigation when a member of the community has been killed. A criminal death must be solved, tried and punished by the criminal-judicial agencies of the community, and the family member has practically no role in the process. We view this loss of control as enormously stressful and this mandated loss of control might further traumatize someone already feeling helpless and victimized by the dying. This group offers an intensive resource of advocacy, support and information to those who are bewildered by the police, the media and the courts. Advocacy during the investigation and trial may come primarily from victim's assistance personnel, but group members may mutually join in advocating for one another during and after the group.

Agenda (10 weekly, two-hour sessions)

Session 1 **Introductions**
The first session begins with the leaders' presentation of group norms and rules of confidentiality. Each member is then encouraged to briefly tell the other members about the dying that brings them to the group
Each group meeting (Sessions 1 through 10) ends with exercises of relaxation and guided imagery.

Session 2   **What is Grief?**
The model of combined trauma and separation distress is presented and the group members are encouraged to present their ways of coping with these distress responses. The leaders clarify resilient capacities and present group and individual exercises for their reinforcement.

Session 3   **Different Ways of Showing Grief**
Male members may be more avoidant in showing their grief, while women members may be more despairing, guilty, and overprotective of surviving family members—and this should be accepted rather than challenged. Violent dying may be followed by possessive thoughts of retaliation, self-blame, and retaliation that may or may not be satisfied by the police and the courts.

Session 4   **Self-Care**
Each group member is finally responsible for caring for his or her own needs. Strategies to improve diet, exercise, calming, and thought diversion are encouraged and definition of comorbid risk factors are emphasized.

Session 5   **The Criminal Justice System**
Translation of legal terms begins and preparations for frustrations of the criminal-judicial process are shared. A representative from the office of police or prosecutor is invited to attend this session.

Session 6   **The Impact of the Criminal Justice System on Grief**
The system needs to solve and punish the dying while the member's grief also needs to honor and remember the loved one. Members are cautioned that the system cannot and will not answer any of their needs beyond the dying and may disregard or disrespect the memory of the loved one. Strategies for maintaining an emotional distance and healthy skepticism regarding the media, police, and courts are encouraged.

Session 7   **Commemoration**
In this session each member presents the memory of his or her loved one through pictures, poems, videotapes, or any memorabilia that enlivens that person's presence within the group. This is an occasion for celebrating the vitality and value of group members' loved ones.

Session 8   **Family and Friends**
Group members invite supportive members of their family or community to join in their insights and progress. This session reinforces continued support within the member's family or community in anticipation of group termination.

Session 9   **Exploring Questions of Faith and Spirituality**
Living beyond the memory of dying and death requires an ongoing engagement with activities and beliefs of value and meaning. A member of the clergy is sometimes included in this session.

Session 10   **Closing.**
A formal group exercise of remembrance for each lost loved one is completed. A final exercise of commemoration for the group and each of its members closes the group.

Restorative Retelling Group

Purpose: For family members and friends who cannot accommodate to images of the violent dying (reenactment) and/or images of self (possession) six months following the death. The primary focus of the group interaction is on moderating trauma and separation distress and reinforcing resilience, before the direct engagement of the group in the imagery of violent dying.

Agenda (10 weekly, two-hour sessions)

Session 1   **Introductions**
The leaders present the norms of the group and rules of confidentiality and clarifies the model of restorative retelling before group members begin their retelling. Each member then tells the story that brought him or her to the group.
Each group meeting (Sessions 1 through 10) ends with exercises of relaxation and guided imagery.

Session 2   **Sources of Support**
Resilience is defined and resources of resilience (personal, family, work, community) are clarified. Each member's concept of death (which may include spiritual beliefs) is explored. An active reengagement with living through activities of value and reconnection with meaningful beliefs is encouraged.

Session 3   **Prevailing Instead of Recovering**
Members cannot expect life to be the same after the violent death of someone they loved. Our objective in prevailing, rather than recovering, is to find a way to live around and through an event that will forever change us. Members are encouraged to talk about these changes.

Session 4   **Comorbidity: Defining Distress and Disorder**
The difference between psychiatric disorders and distress (re-

enactment and possessions) is presented. This is followed by an explanation of restorative retelling and how it moderates distress and possessive thoughts. Since commemoration serves as a basis for restorative retelling, preparation for Session 5 is outlined.

Session 5   **Commemorative Presentations** (4 or 5 members)
Each member has 15 or 20 minutes to commemorate the life of his or her loved one through images, writings, song, or memorabilia and revivify his or her caring role with the deceased before the dying.

Session 6   **Commemorative Presentations** (4 or 5 members)
Continuation of commemoration.
Preparation for death imagery presentations. Members prepare a drawing with crayons or colored pens portraying the imaginary drama of the violent dying. This exercise may be completed outside the group, or as a group exercise if it too threatening for some members.

Session 7   **Death Imagery Presentations** (4 or 5 members)
Each member has 15 or 20 minutes to present and restoratively retell the imagery of his or her loved one's dying. With the guidance of the leaders and other group members they imaginatively reenact their caring role from the commemorative presentation within the dying story.

Session 8   **Death Imagery Presentations** (4 or 5 members)
Continuation of death imagery presentations.

Session 9   **Family and Friends**
Each member introduces supportive family or members of their community to consolidate changes and reinforce post group support in anticipation of group termination.

Session 10 **Ceremonial Goodbye**
A formal group exercise of remembrance for each loved one is completed. A final commemorative exercise for the group and each member closes the last session.

Structure and Organization for CDS and RR Groups

Each session is chaired by two leaders, and invited speakers.
Each session has a separate handout for clarification and additional resources and references
Each session is followed by a written evaluation by the members.
Members cannot miss more than two sessions.
The group may be repeated.

There is no charge for the sessions (our project is supported by Victims of Crime Act funds).

Full descriptions and guidelines of the Criminal Death Support Group and Restorative Retelling Group are contained in written manuals that may be ordered at the following address:

Separation & Loss Service
Virginia Mason Medical Center
925 Seneca Street
P.O. Box 1930
Seattle, WA 98111
Phone: (206) 223-6398

REFERENCES

Adler, A. (1943). Neuropsychiatric complications in victims of Boston's Cocoanut Grove Disaster. *Journal of the American Medical Association, 123,* 1098–1101.

Alvarez, A. (1990). *The savage God: A study of suicide.* New York: W. W. Norton.

Amick-McMullan, A., Kilpatrick, D., Veronen, L., & Smith, A. (1989). *Journal of Traumatic Stress, 2*(1), 21–35.

Bohm, D. (1996). *On dialogue* (pp. 61–68). New York: Routledge.

Bonanno G., & Kaltman, S. (1999). Toward an integrative perspective on bereavement. *Psychological Bulletin, 125*(6), 760–776.

Burgess, A. (1975). Family reaction to homicide. *American Journal of Orthopsychiatry, 45*(3), 391–398.

Breslau, N. (1998). Trauma and post traumatic stress disorder in the community. *Archives of General Psychiatry, 55,* 626–632.

Callahan, R. J., & Callahan J. (1997). Thought field therapy: Aiding the bereavement process. In C. R. Figley, B. E. Bride, & N. Mazza (Eds.), *Death and trauma* (pp. 249–267). Philadelphia: Brunner/Mazel.

Chance, S. (1992). *Stronger than death.* New York: W. W. Norton.

Cote, W., & Simpson, R. (2000). *Covering violence: A guide to ethical reporting about victims and trauma.* New York: Columbia University Press.

Currie, E. (1998). *Crime and punishment in America* (pp. 80–109). New York: Henry Holt.

Damasio, A. (1999) *The Feeling of What Happens* (pp. 61–71). New York: Harcourt.

Department of Health and Human Services. (1997). *Health United States 1996–67* and *Injury Chartbook* (pp .20–30). National Center for Health Statistics, DHHS publication No. (PHS) 97-1232.

Eth, S., & Pynoos, R. (1985). *Post traumatic stress disorder in children.* Washington, DC: American Psychiatric Press.

Eth, S. & Pynoos, R. (1994). Children who witness the homicide of a parent. *Psychiatry, 57,* 287–305.

Figley, C. (1999). *Traumatology of grieving.* Philadelphia: Brunner/Mazel.

Foa, E., Meadows, E. (1997). Psychosocial treatments for post traumatic stress disorder: A critical review. In *Annual Review of Psychology, 48,* 449–80.

Foa, E., & Rothbaum, B. (1998) *Treating the trauma of rape.* New York: Guilford Press.

Foa, E., Keane, T., & Friedman, M. (2000). Guidelines for treatment of PTSD. *Journal of Traumatic Stress, 13*(4), 539–588.

Frank, A. (1995). *The wounded storyteller: Body, illness, and ethics.* Chicago: The University of Chicago Press.

Frank, J. D., & Frank J. B. (1991) *Persuasion and healing* (pp. 40–44). Baltimore: The Johns Hopkins University Press.

Frankl, V. (1959). *From death camp to existentialism.* Boston: Beacon Press.

Frankl, V. (1962). *Man's search for meaning: An introduction to logotherapy.* Boston: Beacon Press.

Freud, S. (1957). Mourning and melancholia. *Standard edition of the complete psychological works of Sigmund Freud,* Vol. 14. London: Hogarth Press.

Gilligan, J. (1997). *Violence* (pp. 191–208). New York: Random House.

Green, B., Grace, M., & Lindy, J. (1990). Buffalo Creek survivors in the second decade. *Journal of Applied Social Psychology, 20,* 1033–1050.

Harvey, J. H. (2000). *Give sorrow words* (pp. 18–38). Philadelphia: Brunner/Mazel.

Herman, J. (1992) *Trauma and recovery.* New York: Basic.

Hillman, J. (1983) *Healing fiction* (pp. 78–81). Woodstock, CT: Spring Publications.

Horowitz, M.J. (1976). *Stress response syndromes.* New York: Jason Aronson.

Horowitz, M. J., Siegel, B., Holen, A., Bonnano, G. A., Milbrath, C., & Stinson, C. H. (1997). Diagnostic Criteria for Complicated Grief Disorder. *American Journal of Psychiatry, 154,* 904–910.

Jacobs, S. (1993). *Pathologic grief maladaptation to loss.* Washington, DC: American Psychiatric Press.

Jacobs, S. (1999). *Traumatic grief: Diagnosis, treatment, and prevention.* Philadelphia: Brunner/Mazel.

Krystal , H. (1968). *Massive psychic trauma.* New York: International Universities Press.

Krystal, H. (1978). Self representation and the capacity for self care. *Annual of Psychoanalysis, 6,* 209–246.

Kulka, R., Schlenger, W., Fairbank, J., Hough, R., Jordon, B., Marmar, C., & Weiss, D. (1990) *Trauma and the Vietnam war generation: Report of findings from the National Vietnam Veterans Readjustment Study.* New York: Brunner/Mazel.

Lakoff, G., & Johnson, M. (1980). *Metaphors we live by.* Chicago: University of Chicago Press.

Langer, L. (1991) *Holocaust testimonies: The ruins of memory.* New Haven, CT: Yale University Press.

Lifton, R. J. (1968). *Death in life.* New York: Random House.

Lifton, R. J. (1976). *The life of the self.* New York: Simon and Schuster.

Lindemann, E. (1944). Symptomatology and management of acute grief. *American Journal of Psychiatry, 101,* 141–148.

Lord, J. (1987). *No time for goodbyes.* Ventura, CA: Pathfinder Publishing.

Malt, U. (1994). Traumatic effects of accidents. In R. Ursano, B. McCaughey, & C. Fullerton (Eds.), *Individual and community responses to trauma and disaster* (pp. 103–35). Cambridge, England: Cambridge University Press.

Marmar, C. (1988). A controlled trial of brief psychotherapy and mutual help group treatment of Conjugal bereavement. *American Journal of Psychiatry 145,* 203–209.

McFarlane, A., Clayer, J., & Bookless C. (1997). Psychiatric morbidity following a natural disaster: An Australian bushfire. *Social Psychiatry Psychiatr Epidemiol, 32,* 261–268.

Meichenbaum, D. (1994). *A clinical handbook: Practical therapist manual for assessing and treating adults with PTSD.* Ontario, Canada: Institute Press.

Murphy, S. (1998). Broad spectrum group treatment for parents bereaved by the violent deaths of 12- to 28-year-old children: A randomized controlled trial. *Death Studies, 22*(3), 209–235.

Murphy, S. (1999). PTSD among bereaved parents following the violent deaths of their 12- to 28-year old children: A longitudinal prospective analysis. *Journal of Traumatic Stress, 12*(2) 273–291.

Neimeyer, R. A., & Levitt, H. M. (2000). What's narrative got to do with it? Construction and coherence in accounts of loss. In J. H. Harvey & Eric D. Miller (Eds.), *Loss and Trauma* (pp. 401–412). Philadelphia: Brunner/Mazel.

Ness, D., & Pfeffer, C. (1990). Sequelae of bereavement resulting from suicide. *American Journal of Psychiatry, 147*(3) 279–285.

New, M., & Berliner, L. (2000). Mental health service utilization by victims of crime. *Journal of Traumatic Stress, 13*(4), 693–707.

Parkes, C. (1993). Psychiatric problems following bereavement by murder or manslaughter. *British Journal of Psychiatry, 162,* 49–54.

Pennebaker, J. (1990). *Opening up: The healing power of confiding in others.* New York: William Morrow.

Pitman, R. K., Orr S. P., & Altman, B. (1996). Emotional processing during Eye Movement Desensitization and Reprocessing therapy of Vietnam veterans with chronic post traumatic stress disorder. *Comprehensive Psychiatry, 37,* 419–429.

Prigerson, H., & Jacobs, S. (in press). Diagnostic criteria for traumatic grief: Conceptual issues, critical appraisal, and an empirical test. In M. S. Stroebe (Ed.), *New Handbook of Bereavement: Consequences, Coping and Care.* Washington, DC: American Psychological Association Press.

Prigerson, H. G., Maciejewski, P. K., Newsom, J., & Reynolds, C. F. (1995). The Inventory of Complicated Grief: A scale to measure maladaptive symptoms of loss. *Psychiatry Research, 59,* 65–79.

Pynoos, R. S. (1987). Life threat and post traumatic stress in school-age children. *Archives of General Psychiatry, 44,* 1057–63.

Pynoos, R. S., & Nader, K. (1988). Psychological first aid and treatment approach for children exposed to community violence: Research implications. *Journal of Traumatic Stress, 1*(4), 445–473.

Pynoos, R. S., & Nader, K. (1990). Children's exposure to violence and traumatic death. *Annals of Psychiatry, 20*(6), 334–344.

Rando, T. (1993). *Treatment of complicated mourning.* Champaign, IL: Research Press.

Raphael, B., & Minkov, C. (1999). Abnormal grief. *Current Opinion in Psychiatry, 12,* 99–102.

Redmond, L. (1989). *Surviving: When someone you love was murdered.* Clearwater, FL: Psychological Consultation and Education Services.

Rinear, E. (1988). Psychosocial aspects of parental response patterns to the death of a child by homicide. *Journal of Traumatic Stress, 1,* 305–322.

Rivara, F. P., & Farrington, D. P. (1995). Prevention of violence. *Archives of Pediatric and Adolescent Medicine, 149,* 421–429.

Rose, G. J. (1987). *Trauma and mastery in life and art* (pp. 182–200). New Haven, CT & London: Yale University Press.

Rosenblatt, P. (2000). *Parent grief: Narratives of loss and relationship.* Philadelphia: Brunner/Mazel.

Rynearson, E. (1981). Suicide internalized: An existential sequestrum. *American Journal of Psychiatry, 138,* 84–87.

Rynearson, E. (1984). Bereavement after homicide: A descriptive study. *American Journal of Psychiatry, 141*(11) 1452–54.

Rynearson, E. (1994, Fall). Psychotherapy of bereavement after homicide. *Journal of Psychotherapy Practice and Research,* 341–347.

Rynearson, E. (1995). Bereavement after homicide: A Ccomparison of treatment seekers and refusers. *British Journal of Psychiatry, 166,* 507–510.

Rynearson, E. (1996). Psychotherapy of bereavement after homicide: Be offensive. *In Session: Psychotherapy in Practice, 2,* 47–57.

Rynearson, E., & Geoffrey, R. (1999). Bereavement after homicide: Its assessment and treatment. In C. R. Figley (Ed.), *Traumatology of Grieving* (pp. 109–128). Philadelphia: Brunner/Mazel.

Rynearson, E., & McCreery, J. (1993). Bereavement after homicide: A synergism of trauma and loss. *American Journal of Psychiatry, 150*(2), 258–261.

Rynearson, E., & Sinnema, C. (1999). Supportive group therapy for bereavement after homicide. In D. Blake & B. Young (Eds.), *Group treatment for post traumatic stress disorder* (pp. 137–147). Philadelphia: Brunner/Mazel.

Shuchter, S., & Zisook, S. (1996). *Biologically informed psychotherapy for depression*. New York: Guilford.

Shear, K. (2001). *Brief psychotherapy of traumatic grief*. Manuscript submitted for publication.

Solomon, R. M., & Shapiro, F. (1997). Eye Movement Desensitization and Reprocessing: A therapeutic tool for trauma and grief. In C. R. Figley, B. Bride, B., & N. Mazza (Eds.), *Death and trauma* (pp. 231–247). Philadelphia: Brunner/Mazel.

Spence, D. P. (1982). *Narrative truth and historical truth*. New York: W. W. Norton.

Spungen, D. (1998). *Homicide: The hidden victims*. Thousand Oaks, CA: Sage.

Van der Kolk, B. (1999). *Traumatic stress: The effects of overwhelming experiences on mind, body and society*. New York: Guilford.

Van der Kolk, B. (1989). Pierre Janet and the breakdown of adaptation in psychological trauma. *American Journal of Psychiatry, 146*, 1530–1540.

Zisook, S., & Shuchter, S. (1996). Psychotherapy of the depressions in spousal bereavement. *In Session: Psychotherapy in Practice, 2*, 31–45.

INDEX